Darkest Secrets of Charisma
Overcome the Lies about Personal Magnetism, Get People to Feel Your Charisma and Influence Others with Your Words

Edition with New Material

from PitchPowerFest.com

Tom Marcoux
Executive Coach – Pitch Coach
Spoken Word Strategist
Speaker-Author of 40 books
Blogger, YourBodySoulandProsperity.com

A QuickBreakthrough Publishing Edition

Copyright © 2016, 2013 Tom Marcoux Media, LLC
ISBN: 061578657X
ISBN-13: 9780615786575

All rights reserved. No part of this book may be reproduced or transmitted in any form by any means electronic or mechanical, including photocopying, recording or by any information storage and retrieval system without written permission from the publisher.

QuickBreakthrough Publishing is an imprint of Tom Marcoux Media, LLC. More copies are available from the publisher, Tom Marcoux Media, LLC. Please write TomSuperCoach@gmail.com

or visit www.TomSuperCoach.com

or Tom's blogs: PitchPowerFest.com   TomSuperCoach.com

This book was developed and written with care. Names and details were modified to respect privacy.

Disclaimer: The author and publisher acknowledge that each person's situation is unique, and that readers have full responsibility to seek consultations with health, financial, spiritual and legal professionals. The author and publisher make no representations or warranties of any kind, and the author and publisher shall not be liable for any special, consequential or exemplary damages resulting, in whole or in part, from the reader's use of, or reliance upon, this material.:

Other Books by Tom Marcoux:
- Year of Awesome!
- What the Rich Don't Say about Getting Rich
- Shine! Don't Let Toxic People Extinguish Your Dreams
- Soar! Nothing Can Stop You This Year
- Time Management Secrets the Rich Won't Tell You
- Discover Your Enchanted Prosperity
- Emotion-Motion Life Hacks … for More Success and Happiness
- Relax Your Way Networking
- Connect: High Trust Communication for Your Success
- Darkest Secrets of Persuasion and Seduction Masters
- Darkest Secrets of Negotiation Masters
- Darkest Secrets of Making a Pitch to the Film / TV Industry

Praise for *Darkest Secrets of Charisma* and Tom Marcoux
- "*Darkest Secrets of Charisma* is a fresh approach so that you can have great influence with people in business and personal situations. Marcoux introduces you to three forms of charisma. Marcoux even shows how introverts can make warm connections that gain results. Get this book and radiate charisma. You'll enjoy your new power and new opportunities." – Dr. JoAnn Dahlkoetter, author of *Your Performing Edge* and coach to CEOs and Olympic Gold Medalists
- "I found it refreshing to see a book on charisma that reveals how to access one's natural gifts to build warm connections. Marcoux shows you how to get out of your own way and radiate natural charm that other people find pleasing and warm. This book will help you inspire people to support you in fulfilling your dreams." – Danek S. Kaus, co-author, *Power Persuasion*

Praise for Tom Marcoux's Other Work:
- "Concerned about networking situations? Get *Relax Your Way Networking*. Success is built on high trust relationships. Master Coach Tom Marcoux reveals secrets to increase your influence."
– Greg S. Reid, Author, *Think and Grow Rich Series*
- "In Tom Marcoux's *Now You See Me*, the powerful and easy-to-use ideas can make a big difference in your business and your personal relationships." – Allen Klein, author of *You Can't Ruin My Day*
- "In *Darkest Secrets of Persuasion and Seduction Masters: How to Protect Yourself and Turn the Power to Good*, learn useful countermeasures to protect you from being darkly manipulated."
– David Barron, co-author, *Power Persuasion*
- "In *Connect*, Tom's advice on how to remain true to yourself and establish authentic rapport with clients is both insightful and reality based. He [shows how] to establish oneself as a credible expert."
- Arthur P. Ciaramicoli, Ed.D., Ph.D., author *The Curse of the Capable*
- "In *Reduce Clutter, Enlarge Your Life*, Marcoux will help you get rid of the physical and mental clutter occupying precious space in your life. You'll reclaim wasted energy, lower your stress, and find time for new opportunities." – Laura Stack, author of *Execution IS the Strategy*

Visit Tom's blogs: PitchPowerFest.com   TomSuperCoach.com

Tom Marcoux

CONTENTS*
These are highlights. Much more is in this book!

Dedication and Acknowledgments	6
Book I: 7 Darkest Secrets—Overcome Lies of Charisma	7
Book II: How to Be a Charismatic Leader	95
Book III: Influence People with Your Words	103
Book IV: Charisma for Introverts (includes: "Flex Your Charisma Power in Media—for Introverts")	111
Book V: Removes Blocks to Happiness, and Charisma Radiates Naturally	125
Book VI: Enhance Your Happiness to Radiate Charisma	137
Bonus: Stop Giving Your Power Away; How to Overcome Self-Sabotage	169,175
Final Word; Excerpt from *Darkest Secrets of Persuasion and Seduction Masters: How to Protect Yourself and Turn the Power to Good*	189,191
Special Offer Just for Readers, About the Author Tom Marcoux, Executive Coach – Pitch Coach	191,197

DEDICATION AND ACKNOWLEDGEMENTS

This book is dedicated to the terrific book and film consultant, and author Johanna E. Mac Leod. It is also dedicated to the other team members. Thanks to David MacDowell Blue, Danek S. Kaus and Sherry Lusk for editing. Thanks to Judita Bacinskaite for rendering this book's front cover. Thanks to Johanna E. Mac Leod for rendering this book's back cover.

Thanks to my father, Al Marcoux, for his concern and efforts for me. Thanks to my mother, Sumiyo Marcoux, a kind, generous soul. Thank you to Higher Power. Thanks to our readers, audiences, clients, my graduate/college students and my team members of
Tom Marcoux Media, LLC – and PitchPowerFest.com.
The best to you.

Book I
7 Darkest Secrets –
Overcome the Lies of Charisma

Chapter 1

What do you want? Now imagine that you could get people to feel your charisma. Can you picture how easily you would get your way?

Charismatic people get what they want—the job, the raise, the customer, and even the "Yes, I'll marry you."

Now consider: What would you do if you could easily influence people with your words?

The power of charisma slammed into my consciousness in high school. Demonstrating initiative as a freshman, I started a movie production club. But soon I was unseated as the president because my best friend had the charisma that sophomores, juniors, and seniors preferred. It hurt.

What did I do? Observing the school had a small TV studio, I immediately started a video production club. I wanted to lead a group of creative young people. Nothing would stop me.

But I always remembered the lesson: *People with the right kind of charisma get what they want and can make a bigger contribution to any situation.*

How did I come to this lesson? I saw that my friend had power and influence to get what he wanted. And it all stemmed from how he talked with people and what persona he projected.

This observation launched my training and study of communication skills. I wanted to get big things done, and I realized that I needed to learn communication on the charisma-level.

With this book, you have the singular opportunity to unleash your ability to radiate charisma. You can start from any point, even feeling extremely shy. I know from experience you can learn skills that create charisma. You can start as I did—a terribly shy nine-year-old boy shaking with terror while playing the piano in front of 31 seniors at a retirement home. So you can move out of the clutches of a difficult past. You can create new and better opportunities in life.

This book is about laying to rest the lies about charisma.

Lie: "If you don't have the charisma of a movie star or a young Bill Clinton or an Oprah, then you're out of the charisma game."

That's not true! Why? Because there are really three types of charisma. You can learn to use what you have naturally.

Here are the three types of charisma:
- Natural Charm Charisma
- Warm Trust Charisma
- Magnetic Charisma

I am NOT talking from theory. I'm talking from personal

experience. Before I get to that, I want to share that **I see ordinary people gain access to their Natural Charm Charisma nearly every week.** How? I teach public speaking on the college and graduate school levels. I help students discover their Natural Charm Charisma and watch them blossom into compelling speakers. I can do the same for you with this book.

Now, here's a bit of my background. My journey has included giving six annual speeches for the National Association of Broadcasters Conferences and teaching public speaking skills to graduate students at multiple schools such as Stanford University. As a CEO, I've led many teams to complete projects from feature films to business books to graphic novels. And I directed a feature film that went to the Cannes film market and gained international distribution. And I won a special award at the Emmy Awards as well as Best Speaker of the Year from Success Builders International. I am also a trained actor who has played leading roles in feature films.

I shared the above to emphasize that you *can* go from fear to empowerment. *You* can learn the skills of charisma. You can go from painfully shy to making big results happen in your life.

What makes this book different from other books on communication is that I go beyond merely listing mechanical techniques you might use. Instead, what follow helps you unleash your *hidden brilliance*.

To do that, you'll need to overcome what I call the Darkest Secrets of Charisma. These arise from "myths" or "lies"—or what many call (mistakenly) common knowledge. These myths paralyze our efforts at radiating charisma. Together we'll dispel these myths. More, we'll learn *countermeasures* so that you can take control of how you influence people.

Realize that many of us usually talk about only one type of charisma. People toss in the names Bill Clinton, Ronald Reagan, Oprah Winfrey, and others. Let's call that form of charisma **"Magnetic Charisma."**

Through this book, we'll not only increase your Magnetic Charisma, but we'll also bring out your own **Natural Charm Charisma.** As I mentioned earlier, there's something that comes naturally to you: Natural Charm Charisma. This is great news for introverts, who make up 40% of the population: *an introvert can shine with natural charm.* I'll show you how.

How is Natural Charm Charisma different from Magnetic Charisma? Natural Charm Charisma is about making the other person feel comfortable in your presence. Some people naturally exude compassion and caring.

Magnetic Charisma is about overwhelming attractiveness. Perhaps you are not blessed with an overwhelming form of attractiveness.

However, you do possess Natural Charm Charisma. In this book, I'll show you how to get obstacles out of your way to expressing this form of charisma, such as nervousness, feeling unprepared, and hesitation.

You'll also learn about **Warm Trust Charisma.** You can do simple behaviors that get people to trust you and feel a warm connection with you. Let's face facts. People hire those they trust. We develop uplifting and influential friendships with people with whom we feel a warm connection.

Here's a quick summary of what we'll cover on the three type of Charisma:

Natural Charm Charisma includes things you can naturally do to make people comfortable in your presence. Your goal is to get obstacles out of your way (like nervous hand gestures) and let your natural charm shine through. *The image: Take a cover off a glowing light bulb.*

Warm Trust Charisma includes things you can do so that people feel that you're genuine and trustworthy. It's all about a warm connection. *The image: Your hand extends in friendship.*

Magnetic Charisma (or Force of Nature) is overwhelming attractiveness. *The image: A magnet pulls people in.*

This book stands out from other books on charisma because it reaches you wherever you are. By this I mean that you can improve upon your situation whether you're already comfortable talking to new people or not.

Charisma does NOT mean

— You must be an extrovert.

— You use words perfectly.

— You copy others who possess charisma.

Instead, you learn to *unleash the charisma power that already resides in you.* When you take action to radiate charisma, you'll get a bonus: You'll feel confident.

In other words, *you act your way to feeling empowered.*

Some people hear the word "act" and think of actors and childhood games of pretending. Drop the idea of pretending. I'm talking about taking action that actually changes your brain. There's a scientific name for this: Neuroplasticity.

The Merriam-Webster Dictionary defines this term as follows:

Neuroplasticity: Capacity of neurons and neural networks in the brain to change their connections and behavior in response to new information, sensory stimulation . . . . Neuroplasticity occurs when neurons in the brain sprout and form synapses. As the brain processes sensory information, frequently used synapses are strengthened while unused synapses weaken.

When you take action, you get new sensory information

both from outside and inside yourself. And as we see above, you change your brain as new synapses form. You'll use this book to change how you go about your daily life. So, in essence, this is not merely a book that you read; *it is a book that you do.* Specifically, you learn to **control your actions and amp up your charisma.**

Let's begin.

Chapter 2:
Darkest Secret #1: You Do Not Need to Feel Comfortable to Look Comfortable and Strong

A professional is someone who can do his best work when he doesn't feel like it. — *Alistair Cooke*

For more than two decades, I have trained people to develop effective communication skills. I've coached thousands of clients, audience members, and graduate students on appearing calm and professional no matter how nervous on the inside. (I founded PitchPowerFest.com.)

One thing remains certain: You do NOT need to wait until feeling comfortable to make a positive even profound impact on others. Unfortunately, many people remain stuck and say to themselves, "I'll do that [give a speech, approach prospective customers] when I feel confident." What they do not realize is many top professionals do not feel comfortable before they step on stage and still do a great job! Considered one the greatest actors of his age, Laurence Olivier reported that he had stage fright before every stage performance. Still, Olivier delivered performances that were compelling and acclaimed by audience members.

The Lie that Inspires This Darkest Secret:

"Charismatic people always feel comfortable before and during an important activity like speaking, networking, or some other social event."

Where does one hear this lie? I've heard it in many conversations when someone would say something like: "Him? He's a natural speaker. I'm sure he doesn't get nervous."

Now, I'm going to explore the three types of charisma and offer a useful method that relates to each type.

Natural Charm Charisma

The word charm does not arise in a lot of conversations, but we do hear something like: "Yes, he's a nice guy." In such a situation, the person radiates a form of charisma that gives the impression of "niceness."

I begin by talking about Natural Charm Charisma because it is something we can all aspire to, even those of us who call ourselves introverts. Some of my clients complain that they're introverts. They emphasize that they're good when talking one-on-one but fall apart when addressing a group.

Natural Charm Charisma Method:

Have a series of one-to-one conversations. First, greet audience members and talk with them before your presentation. Ask them a couple of questions and make a connection. Then, when you give your presentation, talk to the friendly faces in the group. When you speak, give a whole paragraph to one person, and then move on to another friendly face for the next paragraph. In this way, you really do have a series of one-to-one conversations.

This method quiets fear. By focusing on one person, you

are doing something that you do naturally and well. The bonus is that the people behind that person will feel like you're personally addressing them, too!

(You'll get more information on this technique in the section on Darkest Secret #5.)

Warm Trust Charisma

To create trust, it helps to get the "distractions" out of the way. One such distraction is the disconnect between what your words are saying and what your hands are doing.

Warm Trust Charisma Method:

Get your hands away from each other. Another way I say this is: "Don't pet the cat." By that, I'm referring to a nervous person's habit of stroking one hand with the other in a process known as self-soothing. It's as if you're petting your own hand.

Why is it important to avoid nervous gestures with your hands? If the audience sees your hands fluttering about or picking at nails or drumming away at the podium, they naturally think: "What is this person trying to hide? He looks nervous, as if he's scared of getting caught! Caught at what? What is he up to?"

Such thoughts are often on the subconscious level. In fact, their emotional brain has been stimulated. The emotional brain is made of the brain stem and amygdala. This part of the brain focuses on one thing: preventing loss. When you look nervous, your listener's emotional brain and subconscious mind conclude: "What does he have to hide? If he's hiding something, I might get hurt here."

So your answer is to avoid stimulating the emotional brain's defenses in your audience. How? Look calm by keeping your hands away from each other.

As I mentioned earlier, Warm Trust Charisma includes things you can do so that people feel that you're genuine and trustworthy. It's a process of creating a warm connection. And to create that feeling of trust, you need to move your body in a way that is congruent with your words. For example, if you say, "I'm confident that my product can save you $5000," but you're wringing your hands, there is a disconnect between your words and your behavior. So the solution again is to keep those hands away from each other.

How does this tie in with the *Darkest Secret #1—You do NOT need to feel comfortable to look comfortable and strong?* Standing tall while using wide-open hand gestures makes you look comfortable and strong, regardless of whether you're feeling somewhat nervous on the inside.

Magnetic Charisma (Force of Nature Charisma):
Some people come across as a force of nature. They walk into a room, and it looks like they own the place. This comes into play with Darkest Secret #1 when we realize that magnetic people may not feel as confident as they look. There are subtle things that magnetic people do.

Magnetic Charisma Method:
Pause, breathe, and smile. Someone told me once what they noticed when I speak before a group of 600 or more people. They said that I always pause, take a deep breath in, and smile. What does this behavior communicate? Confidence. I know that I'm going to provide valuable information. I know that the audience will have a good time with me. How do I know this? I've rehearsed the speech, gained coaching from my advisors, and studied my craft of public speaking for years.

You don't need to wait for years of experience, though. You can start practicing the pause, breathe, and smile method today.

Why is this technique important? When you smile, you look confident. And the audience responds to you as if you're confident. The positive first impression creates a positive feedback loop. You look confident—>the audience treats you as a confident person—>you feel more confident.

It is easier to act yourself into a better way of feeling than to feel yourself into a better way of action. — O.H. Mowrer

Now that I know about the effectiveness of the pause, breathe, and smile method, I use it on purpose. Even after decades of public speaking, I have times when I feel nervous. In those moments, I decide to pause, breathe, and smile. It calms me down. My deliberate action changes how I feel.

The smile part helps with radiating Magnetic Charisma. Confident people have a natural smile that is welcoming, and it looks like they're really confident! On the other hand, ordinary people may arrive in a room, look around, and frown as their nerves come through. Don't let this happen to you. Practice the pause, breathe, and smile method. When you walk into a room and pause, breathe, and smile, it looks like you own the room. You look comfortable.

Remember, you do not need to feel comfortable in order for an audience to perceive you as comfortable and strong. Practice the above methods, perhaps with a trusted friend or family member.

Practice and rehearsal really count. You might also consider joining Toastmasters, a non-profit organization that provides opportunities to practice public speaking before a supportive group.

Points to Remember:
- **Darkest Secret #1: You do NOT need to feel comfortable to look comfortable and strong.**
- **Your Countermeasures:**

Rehearse methods for expanding your charisma:
1) Have a series of one-to-one conversations.
2) Get your hands away from each other.
3) Pause, breathe, and smile.

Chapter 3:
Darkest Secret #2: You Need to Quiet Your Fear to Unleash Your Full Charisma Power

Successful people I have interviewed are skilled when it comes to fear. They know that they must often be decisive and take action even when afraid.

The Lie that Inspires this Darkest Secret:
"You must eliminate all fear, or you won't be charismatic."

First, let's talk about the difference between this Darkest Secret and *Darkest Secret #1: You do NOT need to feel comfortable to look comfortable and strong*. In many ways, the previous section was about avoiding the appearance of nervousness.

On the other hand, Darkest Secret #2 is about reducing fear—an actual internal process. I'm talking about quieting your fear. I'm NOT talking about eliminating all fear. Why? Because fear, like all emotion, is energy. Fear tells us that something means a lot to you. Learn to harness that energy. Use it to give you an edge. Many actors have revealed, in documentaries and books, that when they lost the edge of fear, their stage performances became lackluster.

But there's a more profound circumstance about fear: Some people allow the discomfort of fear to paralyze them. But this is NOT for you. In this section, we'll cover two mental processes to handle fear.

Handle Fear through Mental Processes

1) Transform Your Perspective on Fear—Convert Fear to Excitement

A Roller-Coaster Story

Years ago, I faced a situation of change or die. Okay, that's overstating the case. But I truly did not like roller-coasters. But my new sweetheart loved roller-coasters.

I once held her hand on a roller-coaster slowly climbing to the top of the first hill. I said, "Whatever happens, know that I love you." She knew then that I was not looking forward to the first drop!

I knew that she would invite me to ride on more roller-coasters, so I had to find a way to become at least somewhat comfortable with them—or just suffer.

I viewed a documentary that revealed that the experience of suddenly going weightless was called "air time." If pressed, I would have called it "heart-in-throat discomfort time."

The next time I stepped on board a roller-coaster, I had a new thought: "This is air time. People like this." Imagine my surprise when I felt my perspective change. I now have two favorite roller-coasters at Walt Disney World: Rock 'N Roller Coaster and Expedition Everest.

What does this mean? And how can you apply it to radiating charisma? Above I demonstrated that a simple new idea can change your perspective—and give you a new experience. When you feel empowered, you can truly radiate charisma. You do not have to stay stuck in fear or discomfort. Realize that a change of thoughts and perspective can give you a new, empowered experience. Your mind is powerful, and it can change your experience of life and tough situations.

Singing a New Song

Carson Daly, the host of the TV show The Voice, turned to a contestant, Cassadee Pope, and asked, "Are you nervous?"

Cassadee replied, "I'm nervous. But it's that nervous-ready feeling." What a great way to reframe the experience of feeling nervous. This is what I mean by "convert fear into excitement."

Cassadee faced the most important audition of her life (up to that moment). She was about to sing for superstars Christina Aguilera, Cee Lo Green, Adam Levine, and Blake Shelton. If just one of them expressed interest in becoming her singing coach, Cassadee would have a chance at performing on The Voice multiple times and a shot at gaining a recording contract.

She could have let her nerves get the better of her; however, she was on top of the situation. She was "nervous-ready." She acknowledged that she felt jittery, but she also affirmed that she was ready! You can do the same.

So what happened with Cassadee on The Voice? She took her nervous-ready feeling and sang so well that all four coaches invited her to be part of their team. She chose Blake Shelton as her coach. Cassadee triumphed through each elimination round and won the competition and was named The Voice!

Remember: fear is energy. Use that energy to fuel your preparation. Tell yourself something like: "Oh, I feel some jitters. That just means this event is important to me." If you have a spare moment, rehearse. Call a friend and practice your answers for a job interview or your opening two minutes of your presentation. If it's too late at night to disturb a friend, call your own phone answering system and record your rehearsal there.

On the other hand, if you're feeling the jitters as you walk up to the podium, tell yourself something like, "I can do this! I've rehearsed it five times this week."

2) Change the Conversation in Your Head and "Make Something Bigger than the Fear"

You may notice that even when you're well-prepared, you're likely to feel some jitters. Your thoughts can either quiet down your jitters or amp them up.

I'm talking about quieting your fear.

This next example comes from the film industry. At the time I'm writing this, the feature film *Marvel's Avengers* became the third top box office film of all time, raking in over $1.5 billion. When that film's director, Joss Whedon, agreed to direct the sequel, he said, "I know I can't match the success of the first one [*Marvel's Avengers*] but I can try to make a better film and that's what I'm excited about. That's the new room of fear I'm entering now."

Let's break this quote down. First of all, Joss changed the conversation in his head. He's not competing to make Avengers 2 win a higher gross at the box office. Instead, he has picked his own target: "to make a better film."

However, he's also admitting that he's entering "a new room of fear." For the first film, he wielded a budget of $220 million. It's likely that Avengers 2 will have an equally substantial budget. That's a big responsibility. He feels responsible to the fans and to his co-workers because a box office failure can hurt everyone involved.

So how did Joss convert his fear into excitement?

He found something that he can make bigger than his fear: His desire to make a better film. Naturally, Joss wanted to work with the characters and actors again. "The question was," he said, "Do I have another thing to say? I was in London and I went to a pub and had some fish and chips and a pint and started writing in my notebook. I'm writing if I was going to do this, what would I say? And 40 minutes later I filled the notebook. So I text my agent and said to make the deal. I'm so in love with that [Avengers] universe and the characters and the way they were played. And I have so much more I want to do with them."

The point we take from the above example is this: You can be charismatic when you make something bigger than the fear. Joss wants to make a better film and work with the Avengers universe and characters again.

I invite you to make your own activity worth so much to you that you'll endure the fear and, perhaps, transcend it. Ultimately, even enjoy it!

When I work with clients to help them hone a speech, I ask them, "What do you most WANT, even long, to say? What will you be really happy to share?" Finding the answers to those questions energizes my clients and gives them something bigger than their fears.

What you want to say is something to move toward, and it functions like a goal. If you don't focus on your goal, fear may propel you away from what you want. Take the time to find out what pulls you forward. This will empower you.

Now, we'll look at specific insights related to all three forms of charisma.

Natural Charm Charisma

Some of my clients who identify themselves as introverts talk about getting so nervous that they're afraid their mind will go blank. Such fear puts a wall between the speaker and audience.

As a remedy, I teach *Recovery Methods.* Here is one you can use if your mind goes blank.

Say, "I'll need a moment . . ."

I encourage my clients and graduate students to pick a phrase to memorize so that they're ready if their mind goes blank. If that phrase can be tailored to different audiences, all the better.

Here are some examples of phrases I've used:

- "I'll need a moment. My train of thought just derailed. I'm looking for a crane."
- "I'll need a moment. My brain needs more RAM." [When I used the RAM line during a speech at IBM, the room rocked with laughter.]

The purpose here is to relieve tension with humor—and to give yourself time to recover your place in your presentation.

You can use one of my phrases, or better yet, come up with your own phrase. One of my college students used, "I'll need a moment. I'm an art student." (His fellow students laughed uproariously.)

The point here is: When you memorize a recovery phrase, you're ready for a potential awkward moment. Your brain works at 700 words a minute, so it is likely that you'll find your place by the time you finish saying your memorized line.

If, on some occasion, you don't immediately find your place, you can say, "I want to emphasize . . ." and mention an earlier point. Or you can go back to the title of your speech and comment on that. Soon enough, you'll recall where you wanted to be in your speech.

Warm Trust Charisma

Each new semester of my college-level public speaking class, I begin with this sentence:

We don't need you to be perfect; we DO need you to be genuine.

I'm telling my students that their goal is a warm and genuine connection with the audience. People do NOT trust a false facade of invulnerability and superhuman "cool." At least not for long.

So an occasional small mistake can actually be a bridge to your audience. If you make a mistake, you can just acknowledge that you're human, and you'll likely connect with your audience more.

Magnetic Charisma (Force of Nature Charisma):

Top professionals do not distract from their message by gushing about any nervousness they may feel. They don't say something like, "Oooh. I'm so nervous to be here in front of all of you!"

Now, advising against "gushing about the nervousness one feels" may seem to contradict the insights I shared in the Warm Trust Charisma section. But the operative word here is "gushing." Acknowledging a small mistake remains different than "wearing nervousness as if it were a medal."

Instead, the charismatic person might say, "I'm excited to share this news with you. I'll need a moment . . . [takes a breath]. Okay. Let's start with . . ."

You can see that change of perspective. Inside, the person may feel fear, but she is telling herself (and the audience) that she's excited. How does this relate to radiating charisma? First, the audience expects you to endorse what you are saying. In a sense, charisma includes a transfer of excitement and interest. Second, it is simply not charismatic to be begging for the audience's mercy as if you're saying (on a subconscious level), "Please, please like me. I'm suffering up here in front of you."

Instead, a professional is excited about the new product that she or he worked so diligently on. And, consequently, the customers want to hear about it.

Here is a fact: Top professionals who exude charisma rehearse a lot.

One extremely vivid example comes to mind. Some time ago, I saw two important political speeches. Clint Eastwood gave a rambling, off-the-cuff speech at the 2012 Republican National Convention. He searched for words, lost focus, stumbled over words, and later admitted that he grabbed a chair at the last minute to use as a symbol of the sitting president. Mr. Eastwood's speech was so painful to watch that I gave up and read a transcript of the speech later. Frankly, it broke my heart because I've appreciated his acting performances and his comments in documentaries on filmmaking.

In stark contrast, for his address to the 2012 Democratic National Convention the following week, Bill Clinton gathered a team and devoted over one hundred hours to research, speech-writing, and rehearsal. His speech came across with warmth and charisma. No one would ever say that Bill Clinton is not a gifted speaker. But here's the crucial detail: he is a well-rehearsed and well-prepared speaker.

I've shared this before, and it's worth repeating: *Any time you feel fearful, rehearse.* Call your phone answering service, and rehearse by recording your spoken words. Rehearse in front of trusted friends. With my clients, I suggest rehearsing at least 9 minutes a day. I like rehearsing near the beginning of my day. Why? I've found power in the practice: Worst first. By the way, even if you rehearse for only 9 minutes, your subconscious mind will work on your speech for the rest of the day!

(Before we go further, here's a word about *Worst first*. I've learned that often the task I might dread is actually the one that will do my career the most good. Also, in the morning, I am fresh so I have more energy to apply to that tough task.)

Each person is different, so it helps when you devote specific attention to your own personal rhythms. Some people come alive in the morning. Others do better in the afternoon or evening.

I don't usually refer to principles of warfare, but this one is pithy and appropriate here:

More sweat in training; less blood in battle.

How does this relate to radiating charisma? The more you rehearse or train with a coach, the more prepared you are. You'll be able to adapt in the moment during a speech. You'll really know your material, and better than that, you will know that you know. That knowing quiets down fear.

Points to Remember:

- **Darkest Secret #2: You need to quiet your fear to unleash your full charisma power.**
- **Your Countermeasures:**

Make the activity worth so much to you that you'll endure the fear and perhaps even transcend it. Take action in the following ways:

1) Transform Your Perspective on Fear—Convert Fear to Excitement
2) Change the Conversation in Your Head and "Make Something Bigger than the Fear"
3) Rehearse and get coaching.

Chapter 4
Darkest Secret #3: You Can Access Your Subconscious Mind through Your Body and Habits—and Move Beyond Shyness

If you feel shy, are you really stuck? No! Act your way into a new attitude.

The Lie that Inspires this Darkest Secret:
"Shy people are stuck. They cannot get better at radiating charisma because they cannot access their subconscious mind and make adjustments."

This false idea holds many people back. They give up and say with exasperation, "Oh. What's the use?! I am what I am."

Really? If we look back at our lives, there are numerous times of "before" which was different than "after." Think of the time before you learned to ride a bicycle. Many of us learned to swim; before that we were non-swimmers.

You learned to read, write, brush your teeth, and more. So settling for "I am what I am" is **not** good enough for you to live with real joy and fulfillment. Before now, you were a person who did not read. Do you think it would have been healthy to stop and say, "I am what I am—and that is a person incapable of reading." No!

Similarly, there was a time before when I performed the behaviors of a shy person. I avoided starting up a conversation with a stranger. I avoided speaking up in a meeting at work. But then I learned to do the behaviors of an effective communicator. I studied, got coaching, and rehearsed. And I took action in real-life settings. Do I still feel nervous sometimes? Sure. But I continue doing the actions of an effective communicator. As one classic book's title exclaims: *Feel the Fear and Do It Anyway*.

So let's dive deeper into this business of shyness. What is shyness exactly?

A definition of shyness at About.com states: "Shyness involves the experience of social anxiety combined with behavioral inhibition. People who are shy are reluctant to express thoughts and feelings, become easily embarrassed, and may experience anxiety symptoms such as blushing."

We see a number of components of shyness:
- internal: a feeling of anxiety
- external: some social behaviors are inhibited
- external: symptoms such as blushing

The key here, though, is the internal aspect. It is the feeling of anxiety that ultimately creates the external manifestations. Conquer the inner, and you'll gain control of the outer.

So how do you conquer that inner anxiety? Hit it where it lives—in the subconscious mind.

The truth is that lasting change requires an impact on your subconscious mind, on that part of your mind of which you are not aware.

If you aren't aware of it, then how do you impact your

subconscious mind? With effective behaviors that you choose.

"Thinking will not overcome fear but action will."
— W. Clement Stone

I have good news. We all possess two tools that can help us "shape up" our subconscious mind:
a) Move Like You're Full of Confidence
b) Shape Your Conscious Thought Patterns

a) Move Like You're Full of Confidence

How do you feel?

In typing that question just now, I noticed that I felt a bit off. So I stood up and did a yoga move of reaching my hands skyward and "opening the rib cage." Now I feel better.

As beings with a physical form, we simply feel stronger when we move better. By "move better," I mean that we move physically in such a way that increases our energy instead of decreasing it. In other words, how we hold our bodies can actually change how we feel. For example, when I slouch while typing at the computer keyboard, I actually block the free flow of energy in my body. However, after doing a good bit of exercise, I feel inspired to jump to the keyboard and write some uplifting ideas to serve my readers.

Now, let's talk specifically about using your body to move from a default-setting of shyness to radiating charisma.

You can feel shy, but move like you're full of confidence.

If you do this, a couple of incredible things can happen. One, you'll start to actually feel more confident. And two, people will treat you as if you were more confident. In a way it's like tennis. If you send out the energy and appearance of confidence, then people "return your serve" with appreciation and positive energy. So the idea is to start feeling better, looking better, and sending out positive energy.

Below are some ways in which you can "move like you're full of confidence":

Feel better through better posture. Imagine a string that comes from the ceiling and attaches to the top of your head. It pulls upward and aligns all your vertebrae so that you sit up straight—or stand up straight. Why is good posture important? When you align your vertebra, you will look strong and charismatic. And better than that: you will likely feel better.

How do I know this? After a car accident, I came under the care of three physical therapists. I learned from them that having my vertebrae aligned means that my muscles exert less energy holding my body erect. They told me the body is designed for the bones to take the weight. Poor posture puts too much of the burden on the muscles, causing an unnecessary energy drain.

What are the consequences for you in terms of shyness and charisma? Charisma requires energy. Slouching drains your energy. Shyness includes feeling "not up" for a social interaction. If you stand with good posture, your recovered energy can be a wall between you and your shyness.

Charismatic people often move in an "effortless manner." People say things like, "She's so comfortable in her own skin." When you align your vertebrae and stand up straight, you become physically more comfortable. When you feel better, you radiate attractive, comfortable energy.

One of the most useful workshops I've ever attended had the delightful name "How to Flirt." I was single at the time and felt I could use some coaching. Little did I know that I'd learn something that would give me poise in all kinds of social interactions. In one exercise, the instructor invited us to lift our diaphragm away from our belly button. By this she meant for us to lift our chest area and stand up taller. With our chest area stretched upwards (a distance away from our belly button), we stood tall, and we looked stronger, and we felt more confident and healthier. And we simply felt more powerful. The important detail is that a physical action can actually change how a person feels. By lifting up his or her chest and standing tall, a shy person can begin to feel stronger and more attractive. And this has a big impact on radiating charisma!

Take Up More Space. People who feel timid close down. They keep their hands in close, their shoulders drooped, and their knees together. They subconsciously try to take up as little space as possible. Unfortunately, this compaction of their body decreases their potential for radiating charisma. I learned a helpful technique from Lynda Obst, producer of *Sleepless in Seattle* (starring Tom Hanks and Meg Ryan) and other hit movies. She said, "Take up more space." By this, she meant make bigger gestures as you talk. You'll even look bigger. And certainly, you'll appear more confident.

So how do you start taking up more space? You can video record yourself giving a speech. You can identify your "minimizing" behaviors and then practice bigger and better ones. You can also engage a coach to help you refine your movements.

Make sure "Heart Faces Heart." Joe Navarro, a former FBI profiler, revealed in his first book that the FBI method of ascertaining truth is a sequence of observations: feet, hands, and face. If your face smiles but your feet point away, FBI personnel are trained to interpret your feet as a desire to "run away." You see, there are two messages. One is on your face, but the agents may feel that it's your feet that are telling the truth.

How does this relate to charisma? If you want people to be positively inclined toward you and to trust you on the subconscious level, then you need to face them—and turn your feet toward them. If you look at someone but do not turn your body so that your chest faces their chest—in the "heart faces heart" position—then the person will not, on a subconscious level, believe that you want to talk with them.

Shy people (or at least, people who are doing shy behaviors) do not fully engage with a person. Their feet often are turned away. Override this behavior. Remember "heart faces heart" and fully turn toward the person.

If you're giving a speech and someone asks a question, turn your body so that "heart faces heart." In that way, you look confident, and you demonstrate that you're giving the person your full attention. Also, if you naturally turn your feet to face the person, this gives the impression that you're not afraid of the person, even if they've asked a challenging (or sometimes insulting) question.

"Heart faces heart" is a prime example of a physical habit overcoming shyness. What happens is that your subconscious mind is observing your thoughts and your body position, and these two elements contribute to how you feel. When you face a person, your body is in a position of strength. Your subconscious mind takes note. Your body, therefore, feels more "on purpose." The more you remain in a powerful posture and behave confidently, the more your subconscious mind believes "I am powerful and I am confident." In turn, because your subconscious mind believes it, so you yourself believe it. And then you act the part!

Do the thing you fear and the death of fear is certain.
— *Ralph Waldo Emerson*

b) Shape Your Conscious Thought Patterns

Take Action to Improve Your Habitual Thought Patterns

Research suggests that a person has thousands of thoughts, and many of them are the same ones day after day. Your thoughts lead to feelings, which often lead to certain behaviors. I call this a Behavior Sequence. It begins with a Trigger—some stimulus in the environment.

For example, "Nadia," the elderly mother of a friend of mine, has what I call an "instant disgust-behavior sequence." When Nadia sees any curvaceous but slim actress on television (her Trigger), she instantly brings to mind her own thoughts about young women and sexual promiscuity. A nasty negativity settles into her chest, which culminates in her saying something bitter and derogatory about an actress whom she does not even know!

Result—anyone near Nadia feels uncomfortable. And all this unpleasantness is unnecessary.

If Nadia decided that she wanted to change her "instant disgust-behavior sequence," she could use the method I share in the following paragraphs. The process is Attach a positive thought to any habitual negative thought. Use repetitions to cement this empowering Behavior Sequence into your daily life. Note that this is not about trying (and often failing) to suppress a negative thought. Instead, you immediately switch the direction of your thoughts. Although you cannot always control every single thought that pops into your head, you can choose what your next thought will be. And with enough practice, just like with tennis or a martial art, your positive, effective move becomes a reflex.

For example, imagine that you accidentally tip over a glass of water. What do you say? Probably something like

"Damn it! Clumsy! Stupid!"

Or do you say something neutral or positive?

I tend to say mildly, "Oh. That's exciting." To me that is a neutral response. In this way, I avoid the negative spiral of self-condemnation. I have, in essence, conditioned myself to under-react to something as trivial as the spilling of water.

Maureen, one of my clients, used to get greatly upset if any of her possessions become creased, dented, or scratched. However, now she says, "It's mine now." That's her shorthand way of saying that the possession has history with her. She gets herself to a neutral place of realizing that her things get dings and dents because she's using them, which probably means that she's enjoying them.

Taking conscious action to improve your habitual thought patterns makes an impact on your subconscious mind. When you learn to shape your thoughts, you gain access to your emotions, which will empower you to radiate charisma.

Let's look at this method in more detail.

Shift Gears: Attach a Positive Thought to a Habitual Negative Thought

We all have negative thoughts from time to time. Often they're triggered by something in the environment. Perhaps, you see a particular car and remember an ex-girlfriend or ex-boyfriend. Then a swirl of upset feelings arises.

Here is the solution: Attach a Positive Thought to a Negative Thought.

For my client Norman, the process looks like this:

Norman's negative thought: "A Honda Prelude. Agh! Sheila drove one of those, and she was cruel about . . . ."

Norman's subsequent positive thoughts: "Stop! I'm free of her. I'm stronger now. I know what to avoid. My life is better now."

In the above example, Norman chooses to focus on how his present moment is better rather than on his past. He does not need to re-experience his past trauma. In essence, he can stop the flood of negative thoughts. Metaphorically, Norman is cutting off the negative thoughts at the pass.

I speak from experience. This method works! Years ago, I had a job at a bank that had nothing to do with my best talents. I felt frustrated that I was losing 8 hours a day to a job in which I could build nothing: no films, no books, and certainly not my own business.

My process looked like this:

My negative thought: "No! Sunday's almost gone. I'll be back at the bank in a few hours."

My subsequent positive thoughts: "I'm grateful for the prosperity of this job. I'll be kind to my co-workers."

Using these positive thoughts prevented me from falling down a spiral of negative thoughts and feelings. Instead of focusing on dreading the routine work, I focused on what was good about the job.

The Advantage of Attaching a Positive Thought to a Negative Thought

Researchers have noticed that emotions appear to last about 90 seconds. When you train yourself to ride out an emotion, you unleash your positive energy. The "Attach a Positive Thought" method helps you get through those 90 seconds and avoid a negative spiral of emotion. How does this help? The best way I can put this is with an example.

Recently, I had a friend, "Nick," who chose to leave my life. This came about when I expressed ideas that were different than his, and he said something intense: "Our conversations are largely useless." They were useless to him because he was not looking for conversation; he was looking for mere agreement.

When a thought about Nick comes into my mind, I can go to a dark place with a second thought like: "Maybe we never had a friendship. Only when Nick thought I was his 'clone' did he actually value me."

That thought will not help me in the present moment.

Instead, I choose these positive thoughts: "We had a good friendship for that chapter of my life. I'm in a new chapter of life, and there's more space for new friends and pleasant experiences."

The "never had a friendship" thought merely causes upset feelings. However, the "We had a good friendship for that chapter of my life" thought helps me ride out the 90 seconds of feeling bad, and then I can go on with my day—free to be positive and productive.

Learn and practice the methods in this chapter, and you'll be able to shape both your conscious and subconscious experiences. Soon, you'll be able to radiate charisma and simply enjoy more of your daily life!

Points to Remember:

- **Darkest Secret #3: You can access your subconscious mind through your body and habits—and move beyond shyness.**
- **Your Countermeasures:**

Practice the following methods to shape both your conscious and subconscious experiences.

Remember that you can change your moment-to-moment experiences by adjusting how you move your body and by mentally "shifting gears." Shyness has much to do with how you feel and the thoughts you think.

1) Move as if you're full of confidence.
2) Feel better through better posture.
3) Take Up More Space.

4) Shift Gears: Attach a Positive Thought to a Habitual Negative Thought.

Chapter 5
Darkest Secret #4: Sometimes Being Vulnerable Increases Your Charisma

People don't care how much you know until they know how much you care — John C. Maxwell

Always appearing strong may prevent genuine connection. Why? It feels fake. Serenity and self-assurance at every moment does not feel human.

The Lie that Inspires this Darkest Secret:
"Never let them see your soft side; vulnerability equals weakness."

Certainly people want leaders who radiate self-confidence. But an audience—whether a single person, a dozen, or ten thousand—listens best to someone to whom they can relate. They feel closer to someone who can relate to their problems. If a speaker comes across as having zero problems, a certain distrust arises. As I write these words, two presidential candidates face each other in national debates. One spent his childhood firmly in the lower middle class, attending public schools. The other grew up in a mansion. Already a large percentage of the voters feel disconnected to one of these candidates. Can you guess which one?

How does vulnerability fit in with the above? To put it concisely, we often can relate to someone whose whole demeanor is: "I went through difficult times just like you. Yes, I'm successful now. But I still remember my roots." A number of charismatic people make a real and strong connection to audiences through a demeanor of "I'm at your side because I have experienced what you have."

Now, here are three methods that help you share your vulnerability and create a better, warmer connection with your audience:

1) Share How You Started Without Knowledge, Money, and Other Resources.
2) Discuss What You Learned from a Mentor.
3) Reveal How You Learned From Failures and Tough Times.

1) Share How You Started Without Knowledge, Money, and Other Resources.

Warm Trust Charisma builds on making a connection. Nearly all top level authors have a "signature story" of how they began with nothing and then through hard work and perseverance rose to success.

The audience wants success, the success the speaker currently has. But if the speaker grew up in a mansion where everything was handed to him, then the audience sees no vulnerability and experiences no connection with the speaker.

We see a real difference between "I'm strong and I've always been that way" and the more useful "I'm strong and prosperous now. But, like you, I've struggled and worked hard to get where I am today."

2) Discuss What You Learned from a Mentor.

No one likes a know-it-all or someone who attributes all of their success to themselves alone. Everyone has help along the way. When you acknowledge the contributions of others, you come across as a real person who is not only vulnerable but also humble.

For example, Robert Kiyosaki, in his 26-million-selling book, *Rich Dad, Poor Dad*, tells the story of the men who taught him the reality of wealth-building. Kiyosaki's "poor dad" was his own father, who worked as an academic and taught him the value of kindness. His "rich dad" was his friend's father, who became his financial mentor and taught him the basics of small business and real estate activities.

By sharing his story, Kiyosaki takes the humble approach. It's like he's saying, "I'm successful, but I didn't get here on my own. I learned my keys to success from my 'dads,' and now you can learn them from me."

The late best-selling author/speaker Jim Rohn always related the story of how he was broke at 24, met his mentor, John Earl Shoaff, at 25, and was a millionaire by 31. He specified how he followed certain principles that Shoaff introduced and took appropriate action to build his fortune.

How does this relate to charisma? Jim Rohn avoided saying, "Look at me! I'm the expert. I was born knowing everything." No arrogance came from Jim. Instead, Jim Rohn's strength came from his connection with the audience and his dash of humility. How did he achieve this? He did not even hint that he had all the answers. He talked about how he grew as a person under the guidance of a great mentor.

Now, I invite you to consider how you can enhance your Warm Trust Charisma by relating stories in which you learned from a mentor.

3) Reveal How You Learned from Failures and Tough Times.

I've learned from giving hundreds of presentations that telling a personal story about what you've learned creates a connection with your audience.

One story I tell goes this way:

"I've learned that you need to keep the main thing the main thing. You need to be vigilant about the most important detail.

I learned this some years ago when I was directing a feature film. This was years before 9/11 [the tragedy of September 11, 2001] when my film crew could still be on a runway at San Luis Obispo Airport. My cameraman needed to get a shot of a two-prop plane with the wing flying over his head. It would be an exciting image with the wing zooming over the camera.

As the airplane raced toward my cameraman, I saw that he was standing too tall and would likely be hit by the wing. The engines were so loud that if I called out, he'd turn to look at me and, BAM, get slammed in the head by the wing!

So I ran over and pulled him down! The wing went over both our heads!

What I learned that day is that you must keep the most important thing in mind at all times.

That day, as the director, I needed to keep everyone safe. I realized that we all need to keep vigilant."

To create a warm connection with your audience, talk about what you've learned, particularly what you've learned from mistakes or failures. Why does this technique work? You exude authenticity when you do that. People respond to truth and candor, and they can relate to someone who isn't perfect.

Every semester, I tell my Public Speaking graduate students: "You are the expert on you." By this I mean that speakers have an advantage when telling a personal story. They saw the situation with their own eyes, and therefore their story will be original.

Too many authors and speakers have repeated the story of a young reporter interviewing Thomas Edison and asking him, "Mr. Edison, how can you continue to try to invent the light bulb when you have failed over 5,000 times?"

Edison replied, "Young man, I have not failed 5,000 times. I have successfully discovered 5,000 ways that do not work and I do not need to try them again."

But wait a minute. What is the accurate story? If you bounce around the Internet, you'll see other numbers like 1,000 or 10,000 failures. And some writers suggest that the discussion was about inventing a battery, not the light bulb. What is the truth? It doesn't really matter because most listeners will tune out the overused story they've heard so many times. To them, it almost feels meaningless.

But when you tell your own personal story, you're sharing something that your listeners have never heard before, something that only you are an expert on.

Be sure to use some version of the phrase: "What I learned that day was . . ." Remember, you create a warm connection by showing that you're human, that you make mistakes and learn from them.

Just a couple of days ago, I learned something new. While teaching my Public Speaking class, I wanted to mime how people get so bored when subjected to a poor PowerPoint presentation that they collapse on their desks. In a flash, I took off my glasses and tossed myself down on the desk. My plan was to avoid hitting the desk by an inch. Unfortunately, with my glasses off, I could not judge distance, and THUD, I whacked my head on the desk.

Head down on the desk, I said deadpan, "Oww. That really hurts."

My students laughed. Mind you I'm not recommending physical self-abuse as a connection tool with others, but I am suggesting that you take advantage of what life offers you. Obviously I wasn't really hurt. I didn't even get a bruise, in fact. But in that moment of surprise, of reaction to the THUD, I found a moment. I took advantage of it and forged another tiny bond with my students.

I rose up and put my glasses back on. I continued, "I learn something new every day! Without my glasses, I couldn't judge the distance to the desk. I'm not going to do that again!"

Earlier in this book, I mentioned: "We don't need you to be perfect; we do need you to be genuine." My point is that we can often be charismatic by being real and approachable to our audience whether it's one person or a thousand. Showing the right kind of vulnerability will increase your charisma, not diminish it.

Points to Remember:
- **Darkest Secret #4: Sometimes being vulnerable increases your charisma.**
  - **Your Countermeasures:**
  1) Share How You Started Without Knowledge, Money, and Other Resources.
  2) Discuss What You Learned from a Mentor.
  3) Reveal How You Learned from Failures and Tough Times.

Chapter 6
Darkest Secret #5: You Do Not Need to Be an Extrovert to Be Charismatic

If you asked a group of people to list the traits that make up a person's charisma, they would undoubtedly include something related to extroversion. They might call that person "outgoing" or "socially adept" or "a people person." The implication is that one must be an extrovert in order to be charismatic.

The Lie that Inspires this Darkest Secret:
"An introvert will never have the same level of charisma as an extrovert."

How can we know what level of charisma a person has? One way is to observe what a listener does after hearing a speaker. An introvert can persuade another person to take action sometimes more effectively than an extrovert. How? It's really about making a warm connection. Sure, an extrovert may appear outgoing. But an audience can relate more, at times, to an introvert who is thoughtful, respectful and really present in the moment with the audience.

Do you feel that you have any characteristics of an introvert? For example, have you ever berated yourself for avoiding a networking event? Perhaps you thought it would be good for you to attend a Chamber of Commerce gathering or a social function after hours at work. But somehow you just felt too tired to go.

I have often berated myself for opting out of such events. But that was before I learned about my "introvert tendencies."

If you ever see a video of me speaking before a group on YouTube.com, you will likely label me as an extrovert. I get people laughing on cue. I speak with energy and conviction. And I do enjoy the "high wire act" of answering audience questions in the moment.

I've discovered, though, that I have an "introvert tendency," namely a need to recharge by having time alone. I've also discovered that I have to build up my energy before giving a speech or attending a networking event—or even going to a party. When I say "introvert tendency," I mean that it is a pattern that a number of introverts demonstrate.

Many popular performers live remarkably quiet lives away from the stage or television. Mike Myers calls himself a "selective extrovert." Steve Martin is famous for his intense privacy. Popular television host Johnny Carson used to describe himself as a loner. This from the man who made his living for decades on *The Tonight Show* talking to people in front of large studio audiences!

The Oxford Dictionary identifies an introvert as "a person predominantly concerned with their own thoughts and feelings rather than with external things."

On the other hand, *The Collins English Dictionary* defines an extrovert as "a person concerned more with external reality than inner feelings." The Collins Thesaurus gives more insight with these suggested synonyms: "outgoing person, mingler, socializer, mixer, life and soul of the party."

Carol Bainbridge, board member of the Indiana Association of the Gifted and noted expert on gifted children, wrote about distinctions between an extrovert and an introvert:

"Basically, an extrovert is a person who is energized by being around other people. This is the opposite of an introvert who is energized by being alone.... Extroverts tend to think as they speak, unlike introverts who are far more likely to think before they speak. ... Extroverts enjoy social situations and even seek them out since they enjoy being around people. Their ability to make small talk makes them appear to be more socially adept than introverts (although introverts may have little difficulty talking to people they don't know if they can talk about concepts or issues)."

What you must remember is that extroversion and introversion are not either-or possibilities, nor are they set-in-stone immutable traits. Most people have a combination of tendencies that can even change over time. In addition, both can be altered through deliberate study and practice.

Some misguided parents say things like: "No, Sarah is shy. She's just not good around people." When little Sarah hears detrimental comments like this one, she internalizes a mindset that can hold her back both in her career and her personal life. She may even start to rigidly define herself as a "shy introvert."

If you had seen me as a child, shaking and embarrassed while playing the piano in front of 30 seniors at a retirement home, you might have called me shy. You might have even said something like, "Him? Speak in front of audiences of 700 people? No way." Thank goodness I did not allow myself to become pigeon-holed by my childhood tendencies.

Now, I use my "shy energy" as a springboard for

empathy with audience members who say they too have introvert tendencies. I also amplify my "extrovert tendencies" to engage audience members in conversation and to improvise humor while I give a speech.

I'm living proof: Introverts can definitely be charismatic. Extroverts may radiate Magnetic Charisma, but introverts can express their Natural Charm Charisma and Warm Trust Charisma. They just need to take that extra step of recharging their batteries before stepping into a social situation.

Here are five helpful methods introverts can use so that they radiate Natural Charm Charisma:

Method #1: Recharge your batteries.

Engaging with other people takes a lot of energy. In fact, some introverts feel their energy dip at the mere mention of an upcoming party. One solution is to get lots of rest. Aim to schedule rest before an event. For instance, if you have an important evening networking event, see if you can avoid scheduling a meeting at work on that same day. Researchers note that one seems to have a fixed amount of willpower for any given day. If you use up your willpower reserve earlier in the day, you won't have enough that night. Introverts in particular may have a limited amount of interacting-with-people energy. Rest up. Limit your exposure to people prior to the event. Focus your energy for that one important event.

Method #2: Do your homework before a networking event or presentation.

A number of introverts report that they like doing research. Look up who will be at the function. Find a biography or articles on the Internet. You'll probably breathe easier with some useful information at your mental fingertips. If you learn something about a new person, you will have a head start on questions you might ask or ways to keep a conversation going.

For larger-scale situations such as speeches and presentations, my clients learn to write a list of *"10 Questions You Do Not Want to Answer."* The next step is to write two answers for each of those tough questions. Extroverts often like to "wing it" and spontaneously answer such questions. Many introverts, though, complain that they do not feel comfortable with improvising. It's best to thoroughly prepare, and then you will have a well of knowledge and rehearsal to draw upon during your presentation.

Method #3: Meet individuals before your presentation.

Introverts tend to say that they do fine when talking to one person. So it's useful to meet a couple of individuals from your audience. That way, when you address the audience, you won't be speaking to a sea of unfamiliar faces; consequently, it may feel less like a formal speech and more like a continuation of earlier conversations with specific individuals.

Here's what I do: Before my speech, I approach members of my audience and say something like "I'm Tom Marcoux. I'm your speaker for today. I have a question. When you first heard about the topic of my presentation, what were you hoping or expecting me to talk about?" After listening to their responses, I ask a follow-up question: "What one subject could I address that would help you the most?"

During my speech, I reference what I learned by talking with audience members. I say something like: "Before my presentation, I talked with a number of you. And Susan mentioned that your team is working on . . ."

Method #4: Have a series of one-to-one conversations during your presentation.

Some introverts find that having to look at the whole group feels like too much. The solution to this problem is to decide where to focus your own attention. Find a friendly face in each area of the room—one on the right, one in the middle, and one on the left. Then address that one person at any given moment. Alternate between the friendly faces you have found. You may find it helpful to focus on the people that you met earlier before your presentation began. An added bonus to this technique is that when you look at one person, the people behind him or her also feel like you're addressing them, too.

Method #5: Give a paragraph to one person before moving on.

One problem I see in my clients and public speaking students is that their eyes jump around too much and too fast. They look like scared rabbits.

In my public speaking class, I illustrate this behavior by quickly shifting my eyes, jumping, and saying, "I see you behind me!" The students laugh at my antics of miming how shifting eyes imply being scared of everyone.

The solution to having "shifting eyes" lies in giving a whole paragraph to one person before you seek another friendly face to talk to. In other words, you're still using the one-to-one conversations mentioned in the previous method; you're just making sure that you focus long enough on one person before moving on to the next.

Method #6: Use questions effectively.

Introverts can radiate a natural charm. How? They listen thoughtfully and take care with their words. They show respect. If done with confidence, all this encourages others to listen and to in turn use their own words with care. Respect given results in respect returned.

How you handle questions is an important part of respect. Here are some techniques you can employ to use questions effectively.

Learn to "catch the question." This is the step you do before you answer a question posed to you. When someone asks you a question, reply with something like:
- "I'm glad you brought that up."
- "George, I can see that's important to you."
- "I haven't thought of it quite that way before. I'll need a moment. I want my answer to be valuable to you."

Researchers report that the human brain operates at about 500 words a minute. People talk at approximately 80 to 100 words a minute. By using phrases like the ones listed above, you give yourself time to make sure you understand the question and to formulate an answer to the question.

Ultimately, you want to find phrases that feel natural to you. You want to vary your responses so that they do NOT sound formulaic. And, of course, don't neglect to actually answer the question.

Develop your own list of "gentle questions." Create a list of questions that you can pose to the audience that they will find easy to answer. Using this technique has two benefits: it makes your listeners feel like active, comfortable participants in the program, and it allows you to control the pace of the presentation.

For example, you could ask the audience something like this:
- "Imagine this situation could resolve itself in the best possible way. What would be part of such a solution?"

You want your questions to avoid putting anyone "on the spot." The last thing you want to do is alienate your audience by making them feel uncomfortable. Remember that close to half of your audience members are probably introverts. This means that they won't respond well to being "in the hot seat."

A good technique, then, is to ask "yes" questions to which your audience can respond by either raising their hand or in some cases by just nodding. If you want to ask a more open-ended question, make it an easy one. In other words, toss your listeners a nice, slow lob that they can hit out of the ballpark, not a wicked slider that makes them look foolish.

Using well-placed questions has an added bonus: they give you small "breathers" throughout your speech. While your audience is busy answering your question, you have a bit of time to line up your next thoughts.

A Note about Warm Trust Charisma

Certain actions create a warm trust between you and the audience. Asking gentle questions helps. Listening carefully demonstrates your care and concern for your audience. Saying back what you heard gives evidence that you were indeed listening.

Realize that introverts have many natural skills: thoughtfulness, attention to detail, and clear thinking about issues and concepts. They are also quite capable of radiating charm and creating connections without having to reinvent themselves as extroverts.

Avoid giving up on developing your own charisma because you don't consider yourself to be an extrovert. Instead, make the most of your own natural tendencies.

Points to Remember:
- **Darkest Secret #5: You do NOT need to be an Extrovert**

to be charismatic.

- **Your Countermeasures:**

The following methods help introverts enhance their personal energy and make the most of their "introvert tendencies." When that happens, the introvert can radiate Natural Charm Charisma.

1) Recharge your batteries.
2) Do your homework before a networking event or presentation.
3) Meet individuals before your presentation.
4) Have a series of one-to-one conversations during your presentation.
5) Give a paragraph to one person before moving on.
6) Use questions effectively.

Chapter 7
Darkest Secret #6: You Need to Quiet Self-Doubt to Unleash Your Full Charisma Power

Ever see someone give a speech with total confidence and warmth and then say to yourself, "I couldn't be that good"? You're not alone. Many people react the same way—with a deluge of doubt.

This process of self-doubt actually consists of two stages: comparison and prediction.

Let's begin with comparison. Author and artist Hugh MacLeod wrote: "Never compare your inside with somebody else's outside." Comparing ourselves to someone else is tricky business. For one thing, it's difficult to do without feeling inadequate when it's over. Secondly, it's often flawed by inaccurate information that we ourselves generate. We see that confident person on the stage, and we assume that it must all come so easily to him. What we don't see is the hours of preparation that got him there or the waves of stage fright that he had to calm before walking up to that podium.

Comparing ourselves to others inevitably leads us to self-defeating prediction. We basically create a negative self-fulfilling prophecy, which drains our energy and our will to take action. We see someone excelling at what we aspire to, and we tell ourselves that we could never be that good. As a result, we never even try.

I'm not saying that charismatic speakers never lack faith in themselves. Quite the contrary. The difference is they know how to handle those occasional moments of self-doubt.

The Lie that Inspires this Darkest Secret:
"A drop of self-doubt dooms anything we try to achieve."

This false idea causes so much damage. The truth is that many professionals who radiate charisma often feel nervous before important events. For example, Bono, lead singer of the band U2, reveals that he always feels nervous on the morning of a concert—and he's been singing at thousands of shows over the years.

The best speakers know enough to be scared... the only difference between the pros and the novices is that the pros have trained the butterflies to fly in formation. — Edward R. Murrow

Unlike their timid counterparts, charismatic people communicate powerfully because they reshape their experiences with self-doubt into something positive. They do this by practicing compassion—for their listeners and for themselves.

Practice Compassion for Your Listener

At the beginning of each new semester, I have my Public Speaking students form two lines; they stand across from their partner for an exercise. During the exercise, they hold up a pen while addressing their partner on the other side of the room. "This is a pen," they say before walking over to the other person, "and this is for you." Then they give the pen to their partner.

After the exchange is repeated in the other direction, the students return to their seats, and I ask them what purpose the simple exercise had.

"We learned to project our voice."

"We learned to focus on one person."

"We gave something to an audience member."

I agree and emphasize: "Your speech is a gift. You give it like you gave that pen."

When you focus on the benefits that you're giving to a listener, you are exercising a form of compassion.

If you want others to be happy, practice compassion.

If you want to be happy, practice compassion.

— The Dalai Lama

What is compassion? *The American Heritage Dictionary* defines compassion as a "deep awareness of the suffering of another coupled with the wish to relieve it."

The more you focus on serving your listeners, the more your self-consciousness (and self-doubt) falls away. Why? You've directed your attention in a positive way—away from yourself and onto your listeners.

Several years ago, I learned how to quiet my discomfort about going to a networking event. I learned to tell myself, "I'll listen well and the new person will enjoy talking. I'll ask gentle questions to get the other person talking."

So, attending the event and meeting other people was not about me; it was about them! I put the metaphorical spotlight on others. By listening to them, I allowed them to bask in that spotlight.

Turn from "How Am I Doing?" to "How Are You Doing?"

When I was a young boy playing piano in front of 30 seniors, I shook with terror. Filled with self-doubt, I feared that I'd make mistakes and the elderly audience member would judge me. My leg fluttered so badly that I was afraid that my foot would slip off the piano's sustain pedal. Such an action would create a loud, embarrassing THUD.

I was in the clutches of thinking, "How am I doing?!"

After hundreds of presentations, my focus is now on "How are YOU doing?" I focus on benefits for my audience; in that way, I extend compassion to my audience. I ask questions and listen carefully to their responses. A friend asked, "Tom, how did you get to that frame of mind?" I replied, "I discovered that when I focused on serving the audience I went from self-focus and fear to connecting with audience members and being excited about the interaction."

Practice Compassion for Yourself

Although it's important to have compassion for others, you must also have compassion for yourself. Why? It's part of putting yourself at ease, and a charismatic person radiates ease and confidence.

Compassion means identifying your own pain, finding your own tender spots, learning your own weaknesses. Then, like a tennis player who knows he has a poor backstroke, you apply yourself to improving those weaknesses. Is this easy? Often, no. Not at all. Many of us still recall damaging criticism from parents, guardians, teachers, and other authority figures. We need to unlearn or set aside those hurtful ideas that were acquired from others, such as "You're not good at this." or "Joey is a shy person."

How does this tie in with charisma? If you continue to believe you are that "shy person" who is "not good at this," your body language will follow suit. You will look timid and not charismatic. However, if you proactively redirect your negative thoughts, you will radiate ease and confidence.

So how do you that? By being kind to yourself by reshaping your inner dialogues. It might look something like this:

- "I'm not good at this, and I never will be."
- "Stop. That's just an idea left over from Mrs. Smythe in 8th grade. The truth is that I've worked hard to make this better and I'm definitely improving."

You can see how saying "stop" and assuring yourself of your actual progress can place you into a better state of mind. This is a start towards extricating yourself from the clutches of self-doubt.

Reshape Your Self-Doubt with "Instant Reframing"

To unleash your Warm Trust Charisma, it helps to unclog your thinking. Many people get stuck in tongue-lashing themselves. How they can revise those detrimental habits? By changing their behaviors and thought patterns so that they avoid stirring up self-doubt.

Researchers have observed that timid people tell themselves ideas that make things uncomfortable. They have a mind-chatter of "They won't like me." or "I'll screw it up." Repeating ideas like these raises self-doubt until it is like a sergeant yelling at a new recruit.

Our solution is to use something called an Instant Reframe.

Warm Trust Charisma Method: The Instant Reframe

Human beings frame (or limit) their view of the world in any given moment. Picture this. Two people attend a party and compare notes in the car on the way back home. Imagine this dialogue:

Serena: "What a great party! People were telling jokes and

having fun."

Jack: "What party were you at? Didn't you see that married couple endlessly arguing next to the aquarium?"

Who's right? They're both right in a way. But they drew their conclusions based on what they saw in their limited perception or their "frame."

When we reframe a situation, we see it with new eyes.

Practicing reframing forms a foundation for changing yourself for the better. In his book, *The Power of Habit*, Charles Duhigg, cites research data in which it was discovered that a person can reframe a situation and change behaviors. Once the person puts in new behaviors, the neural pathways in her brain are overwritten.

One test subject, Lisa Allen, dropped 60 pounds, ran marathons, and completely improved her career and financial situation. Before that, she felt miserable about her heavy body and financial troubles. But her transformation started with just one insight. Her transformation began when she followed a new intuition that she wanted to walk in a desert on a future vacation. She realized her first step would be to quit smoking. She then dropped overeating. The big discovery was that her brain still had sections that responded to food and smoking but the addictive responses had quieted down. New neural pathways had grown in her brain and were more powerful than the old, addictive pathways.

This may sound like the process was easy for Lisa Allen. No. But the transformation process began in a simple way. One insight. One commitment. One big desire that was more important than the patterns she had been living.

And that's what I'm talking about with one method: reframing. Again, reframing is about seeing a situation with new eyes. You make a conscious choice about how you will interpret a situation or event. Imagine how reframing can change the experience of making a mistake while giving a speech.

Margie tells herself: "Damn! I said the wrong number. I'm so stupid."

In contrast, Trudy tells herself: "Oh. I made an error. I can fix this."

Do you see the two different frames? One is "Mistake equals 'I'm stupid.'" The other one is "Made an error. I can fix this." Even the word "error" has less of an emotional charge than "mistake."

My point is that you can clog yourself up with self-condemnation which fuels self-doubt. This puts up a wall between you and the audience. Why is this important? When you're full of self-doubt and self-condemnation, you naturally want to step back from what you perceive is causing the pain: the audience. In fact, many of the clients and graduate students literally step back from the audience. Their body expresses their inner turmoil. And the audience senses this standoffishness.

On the other hand, if you have an Instant Reframe of "Made an error; I can fix this" you feel empowered. And you stay close to your audience. One related technique I share with my graduate students is to recover after an error in a speech with: "That's not what I mean to say. What I meant to say is . . ." You acknowledge the error and immediately fix it.

Use an Instant Reframe to help for rehearsals:

Gina says: "Another day, and I didn't rehearse my speech. I'm such a [fill in self-criticism here]. . ."

Instead, Gina could use this Instant Reframe:

"Before now, I didn't rehearse.

But now I can call Cindy and rehearse the opening 2 minutes of my speech."

The pattern is:

"Before now, I did not ____.

But now I can [positive action.]"

You let go of self-recriminations. You guard your personal energy and keep an even or positive mood. And with positive energy you can actually take action and improve your performance. This can quiet down self-doubt.

Learn the power of "Don't compete; create."

You have natural brilliance inside you. One target of this book is getting rid of those distractions interfering with brilliance. Think of it as cleaning the glass of the lamp that is you.

At the beginning of this section, we discussed the negative statement: "I can't be that good."

The truth is: You can be good—and in your own way.

One of my clients, Mira, an up-and-coming speaker, came in complaining that she was nowhere near as good as Anthony Robbins. Now Robbins is one of the highest paid speakers of all time. He's loud, he's massively tall, and his passion gushes from every pore. Thousands of people like his work. He has the audience sizes to prove it.

However, a number of people have told me that they do not like Robbins. Why? Some say, he's too loud, too brash, and too flashy in his approach.

I shared this information with Mira and gave her an Instant Reframe: "Don't compete; create."

Think of it. Not everyone likes Robbins. And he cannot be everywhere! So there is plenty of space in the speaking world for Mira. She does not compete with Robbins. She creates her own form of connecting with her audience. From observing her speeches, I know that when she answers questions and has a dialogue with the audience, they really feel her compassion and kindness. That's her special talent.

Now, with this different frame of reference (created by an Instant Reframe), Mira can quiet down her self-doubt. She is not in competition with Robbins. She remains in the process of creating her personal ways of expressing her truth.

Take Care of Yourself

Showing compassion for yourself is not just about reshaping your thoughts. It's also about taking care of your own emotional and physical needs.

Neglecting your own needs can cause a lot of trouble. For example, you may feel tired and overwhelmed, and your romantic partner forgets to do a chore like getting the dry cleaning. Suddenly, you find yourself deeply upset. Later, you realize that your upset was out of proportion to your partner's mistake. You were simply exhausted due to lack of rest.

So what is the solution? The idea is to take care of yourself so that you do not fall to a low mood—or that you do not stay in a low mood for too long.

Now what is a low mood? Imagine a chart. Imagine the numbers 0 to 100 on a vertical line. If you're above 50, you're in a relatively high or positive mood. 50 can stand for "I'm okay." Below 50 and you're in a low mood. On occasion, a friend will tell me that he's "negative 20." That's a really low mood!

Of course, we all feel low at times. What does this have to do with radiating charisma? The big difference about charismatic people is this: Those who radiate charisma have devised ways to feel energetic when they need to. Sure, some charismatic people may be able to naturally "switch gears." But others have to work at it; they must do in private what it takes to be energetic when they're in public.

Magnetic Charisma (Force of Nature)

Charismatic people are full of energy. Many of them just seem to vibrate on a fast moving level at all times. However, even they often do things to keep up their energy. For instance, they might make sure to be around people who genuinely support them.

To love a person is to learn the song that is in their heart and sing it to them when they have forgotten. — Thomas Chandler

Supportive people say things like: "I know you can do this. You just need a little more rehearsal. But get some rest now. You have put in a good day's work."

Charismatic people also take responsibility for recharging themselves.

What do you do for yourself to recharge? My clients have mentioned activities like these:
- "I soak in a hot bath."
- "I put on soothing music and assemble a puzzle."
- "I go to yoga class every Tuesday."

Magnetic Charisma Method: "Two for You"

Many of us feel that we're so busy that there is "no time for doing something just for me." This is a symptom of what might be called a "false economy." By not taking care of yourself, you may think that you're saving time. But you're not because you're setting yourself up for a fall—or at least something like a cold or other illness.

Instead of doing that, identify two things that you can do to support yourself each day, and then do those things. For example, every night before I go to sleep, I write down my

Six Top Targets for the next day. These targets are broken down into "2 for You; 2 for Work; 2 for Family." These are the six vital tasks that will ensure that the next day is a successful one for me.

Most people are good at the two work targets or the two family targets or possibly even all four of those. But many fail miserably at the two "you" targets. Don't do this to yourself. Learn to take care of yourself as much and as well as you take care of everything else.

Make a point to do two things for yourself that keep up your own energy. For instance, I exercise every day. That's one. And I watch something (video clip, digitally recorded TV show) that gets me laughing. Every day. Without fail.

Here are some things that my clients have identified that renew their personal energy:

- "I read for at least half an hour each day."
- "I get up a little early and have a ten-minute meditation in the morning."
- "After work I go to a quiet room and work on my novel for 30 minutes before I join the family activities."
- "I take a walk at lunch time every workday."

What can you do to keep up your own energy?

What does renewing your personal energy do for you related to charisma? It gives you a big storehouse of energy. Let's face it. Charismatic people radiate energy. To do the same, you must first have such energy within yourself.

Self-Care and "For the Team"

In coaching people for decades now, I see something over and over. Some individuals will do more for a family member than for themselves. I call these "for the team" people. If you find that you will do more for other people than yourself, I invite you to consider self-care as integral part of your "for the team" mentality—whether your team is your loved ones and or your co-workers.

Let's face it: If you're cranky and miserable, you bring everyone down. You lower their quality of life. And more, you lower your own productivity. Everyone loses. However, if you take care of yourself so that you're not cranky and miserable, everyone wins, including you.

In recent years, I have learned to stay aware of my own state of being. I notice when my metaphorical gas tank is running low. In the past, I would just press on or "soldier on." But then I was susceptible to being irritable. Now, I make sure to take care my own needs for rest and recuperation. My own family tells me that I'm much less stressed out than several years ago even though I face more stressful work details now than I did then. It's all because I'm more careful to keep myself strong and positive.

Use Rehearsal and Coaching to Quiet Self-Doubt

Now, let's talk about rehearsal for a moment. The more rehearsal you do, the quieter your self-doubt will be. Remember, too, that rehearsal can at times be a playland where you discover new ways of expressing yourself. For example, in his later years, Winston Churchill dictated his speeches. He often discovered a new turn of phrase by speaking his first ideas out loud.

But how much rehearsal is ideal? One principle I share with clients is: Anytime you feel nervous, rehearse. By this I mean, instead of sitting there upset, rehearse some portion of your presentation. Call a friend and ask to rehearse the opening two minutes of your speech. If it's late at night, you can call your own phone answering system, and rehearse using that device.

Consider video-recording your rehearsals. These are especially useful because you can see where you need to improve. If you're overwhelmed with concerns, you may want to engage a public speaking coach—even for just an hour. You can make big strides when someone shows you how to raise the level of your game.

Take Rehearsal up a Notch with Coaching

Coaching can identify where you are improving and where you may still need improving. In this way, coaching raises the value of your rehearsal. Here are some concepts to consider when employing a coach:

What makes a good coach?

The good coach encourages you to stretch, to take the extra step to accomplish what you want to accomplish.

Young people need models, not critics. — John Wooden

A good coach encourages you and avoids cutting you down. He says things like, "That's good, but I know you can do better."

When I coach speakers, I begin with "what works" and get them to value what they have already accomplished. Then I move on to "areas to improve."

What makes a bad coach?

A bad coach is so full of his own ego that he does not have room for you. If someone badgers you in an unhealthy way, find another coach.

What kind of relationship should you have with your coach?

An honest one. For example, I invite the editors of my books to hold nothing back. Sometimes, when I'm going through my editor's notes on my manuscript, I feel like a punching bag. I work on the manuscript for a while and then take a break. Later, I come back and face her remarks that push me to improve my writing. I do not expect to be coddled. I focus on getting better at my craft.

What is your responsibility to your coach?

To push yourself. In order to get the most from coaching, get clear in yourself. Answer this question: Do you truly want to improve at your craft? If you say a heartfelt "yes," then devote your committed effort. Be coachable. Listen carefully. Ask questions and find opportunities to implement your coach's suggestions. Take action. Then return to your coach and report your progress. Expect to confront your insecurities and to press on so that you accomplish better work.

Finally, your work is yours. If you're doing artwork or writing, make sure to maintain your own voice. As author Julia Cameron wrote (paraphrased), "Original means you are the origin of the work."

* * *

As we come to the close of this section, I want to leave you with restatements of two empowering insights:
- When you focus compassionately on your listener, then your self-consciousness and self-doubt fade away.
- When you are compassionate toward yourself and take care of yourself (including rehearsing enough), then you have the energy to radiate charisma.

Points to Remember:

• **Darkest Secret #6: You need to quiet self-doubt to unleash your full charisma power.**

• **Your Countermeasures:**

Focus on these areas:

• Demonstrate compassion for your listener. Focus on "How are YOU doing?"

• Demonstrate compassion for yourself ("2 for you")

Chapter 8
Darkest Secret #7: People are Attracted to Those Who Are Vibrantly Alive

Have you noticed that charismatic people seem unusually attractive? But if you really pause and make careful observations, you'll notice many of them are not, in a physical sense, extraordinarily attractive.

The Lie that Inspires this Darkest Secret:
"Only certain types of people can be attractive—those who have a movie star appearance."

When this false idea is internalized, people may exhibit one or more of the following behaviors, which are decidedly uncharismatic:
- Shrinking or hiding
- Slouching instead of standing straight
- Refusing to make eye contact
- Choosing to stand where they feel least noticed
- Never volunteering
- Speaking in a low, soft voice which is often nothing at all like their normal tones.

- Wearing nondescript ties or other such clothes
- Choosing what others do at restaurants
- Buying lovely jewelry but rarely wearing any.

These people may feel intimidated by someone who seems to have overwhelmingly positive gifts, such as physical attractiveness or a resonant voice. They may think of themselves as unattractive and feel shame as a result. All of this causes them to want to make themselves invisible.

Here's the truth: Anyone can learn to make the most of what they already possess—and many don't realize just how valuable that might be.

Ever notice people who seem attractive in person but a photograph just does not capture their allure? In many cases, photographs simply cannot reproduce what makes them so dynamic, so interesting, so compelling—their "aliveness." It's the aliveness that makes them seem so attractive because they radiate energy.

Here are six methods to demonstrate how vibrantly alive you are. They're called the S.W.I.T.C.H. process:

S – Set up a Switch Phrase
W – Wonder about the "fullness" of the other person
I – Inquire with positivity (ask empowering questions)
T – Take time for quiet and compassion
C – Check out the D.E.C. Advantage
H – Honor the moment

I realize that above I'm introducing some new terminology: "switch phrase," "fullness of the other person" and the "D.E.C. Advantage." Continue with me through the next paragraphs, and these new terms will become clear.

First, I'm using the word "switch" because often we can switch the direction of a thought pattern that threatens to shut down our Natural Charm Charisma.

1) Set up a Switch Phrase

Researchers suggest that people have up to 15,000 thoughts a day. The problem is that many, if not most, are repeated, negative thoughts. Most come from one's conditioning as a child.

Many people report that they criticize themselves a lot, often with a variation on comments from parents, guardians, and teachers gave them as they grew up:

- "Damn it! You did it again. When will you ever learn?!"
- "Clumsy!"
- "Stupid!"
- "No, don't even try! You'll break it!"
- "I'm not choosing you, so put your hand down."
- "Well, what do you want me to do about it?"
- "Just go away, get out of my sight!"

Children are still learning self-control, and they often try the patience of adults. For that reason, they end up receiving a lot of negative feedback. All too often in our society, they don't get enough positive feedback to balance it out. Disparaging remarks begin to feel like the norm. Our failures and faults from childhood become the premises with which we lead our lives.

Those disparaging remarks and the emotional chaos that they cause can torpedo one's natural charisma.

Here's a solution: Something I call a *Switch Phrase*. These are words that alter the direction of your thoughts. What you do is memorize certain phrases that empower you. Then, just before an event when you need to radiate charisma, you can repeat them in order to energize yourself.

Energizing yourself is not lying to yourself or pretending.

It is unleashing something that is already present inside of you. Call it your "positive potential." I often call it "natural brilliance." Some people consider it to be their "higher self."

Here are some examples of empowering Switch Phrases:
- "I've got this!"
- "I can do this!"
- "This is something that I do!"
- "Talking and radiating charisma is something I do!"
- "I'm helping him and he can sense that!"

Use a sheet of paper or a page of your personal journal and write down your own Switch Phrases. You can gain even more power by attaching a motion to your Switch Phrase. For example, some of my clients tap their fist on their thigh while saying, "I can do this!" The combination of words and movement ignites empowering emotions and sparks passion—passion about what you can and will accomplish.

2) Wonder about the "fullness" of the other person

Have you noticed that some people are quick to judge everything? They say things like:
- "Oh, the duck is more tender at the other restaurant."
- "Her? She's one of those newly rich people with no taste."
- "He has no class. What a disgusting man."

Such judging seems to be a reflex in human beings. It just comes so easily to us. In fact, some researchers note that people can make about 15 judgments about a stranger in only four seconds!

Have you ever looked at a friend and thought, "I know what he's going to say"? We all have done this. The truth is our friend is NOT exactly the same today as last week or last month. But our "automatic judging reflex" thinks we know what the friend will say. Sure, sometimes, we're right about what the friend actually says, but perhaps the words feel different in this present moment. For example, if I said six months ago, "My father is bitter," I may have been speaking from simple irritation. However, if I say the same thing today, it may be more like "My father is bitter. It's so sad. I know he loves me, but he just does not know how to express it. I wish we could have the close relationship that I've seen others have with their fathers." So now the words, "my father is bitter" are not about irritation; they're really about grief.

My point is that we need to put our instant-judging reflex on hold. Why? It limits our possibilities. When we instantly judge someone, we radiate a negative energy that he picks up on. Then we can't take in the "fullness" of that person. We end up letting a particular detail blind us to what is good or even admirable in him. It's too easy to judge a new person by clothing or a mannerism. For example, a disheveled man looking like a mechanic came into a bank. A clerk instantly judged him as a low-income person. She refused to cash a check for him. Some minutes later he withdrew millions of dollars from the bank as his reaction to the poor treatment.

To radiate Warm Trust Charisma . . . Switch from instant judging to wondering:

- Wonder about the virtues of the person in front of you.
- Wonder about how he makes a positive difference for someone in his circle.
- Wonder how you can make a warm connection with him.

This switch from judging to wondering opens you up to "be in the moment." You free yourself from the prison of a limited perspective, the prison of bias and presuppositions. We often miss something good in someone while we're distracted by some surface trait. Our fixation on this outside attribute prevents a warm connection with that person.

The truth is: people can feel our contempt. And it's far too easy to fall into contempt if we're judging a person on one or two characteristics. That's why I'm inviting you to become a "positive detective." Look at the faces of your audience and see what they respond to. See where you and a listener connect.

Occasionally, one of my college students has serious frown on his face. Is he upset with the material I'm presenting? Could it be that he had a fight with his romantic partner or roommate and lost a lot of sleep? Or wait—he could be concentrating on what I'm saying! Many times the frowning student will suddenly turn around and laugh at a joke or funny story that I've shared.

Here's another principle that goes along with switching from instant judging:

Stop trying to impress; instead be impressed with the other person.

Again, this is all about "wondering" about the positive characteristics of your listener. My clients learn to ask questions of their audience and to watch faces to see what people respond to. As my clients express sincere attention for their audience, they radiate Warm Trust Charisma.

3) Inquire with positivity (ask empowering questions)

Just as it's important to "switch" from negative thoughts to positive ones, it's also critical to utilize empowering questions. An empowering question is one that guides the direction of our thoughts and feelings toward having more personal, positive energy. For example, an empowering question can be "What are you grateful for?" or "What is good in your life at this moment?" Such questions can switch the direction of our thoughts. With empowered thoughts and feelings, we radiate charisma.

With downer thoughts, though, we shut down our Natural Charm Charisma.

What is a downer question? Something that drags your energy and even your estimation of yourself to the depths. Here is one: "Why does this always happen to me?"

You might notice some people when winning a prize say, "Oh, I never win anything!" Well, that is literally not true. They are in that very moment winning a prize.

Other people say that they're not good at remembering names. And then they live that self-fulfilling prophecy. Now wait a minute, aren't some people truly not good at remembering names? Yes. But the story does not have to end there. I have worked with a number of people who have chosen to learn the methods of remembering names and have been surprised at their levels of improvement. What was different about these people? Their starting point. They held a small hope that they could get better at recalling names. I call this "being an optimistic realist." Optimistic realists have an advantage. They begin with a hope, and they're willing to work to make that a positive outcome.

Now, I invite you to create empowering self-fulfilling prophecies. How? By asking yourselves empowering questions.

Author Noah St. John asks a powerful question, "Why is it easy for me to be rich?"

In answer this question, Mina, one of my clients, said: "Because I'm good at attracting top quality team members and together we make high value and popular products."

What is the value of asking and answering such a

question? First, it puts you into a better mood. Secondly, it can give you a to-do list.

From Mina's above response, she encourages herself to do three things:
1) attract top quality team members
2) work together to make high value products
3) make the products (through excellent marketing) popular with buyers.

Now, to radiate charisma during a presentation, ask yourself this question before you walk on the stage: "Why am I ready to give a great speech?"

Then answer yourself with responses like these:
- "Because I have rehearsed at least 9 minutes a day for the past 10 days."
- "Because I hired a speech coach who helped me warm-up my stories."
- "Because I'm excited to present my 'airplane story' and I know from experience the audience will enjoy it."

Use empowering questions to "inquire with positivity" and watch your charisma soar!

4) Check out the D.E.C. Advantage

Authors and researchers, including Stuart Brown, M.D., emphasize the vital role of "play" for both brain development and the invigoration of one's soul.

Three elements of play come to the forefront, which I call the D.E.C. Advantage: Discovery, Exhilaration, and Challenge.

Discovery

I invite my clients and college students to "find your

smile somewhere during your speech." I want them to find something they will ENJOY sharing with the audience, something that will literally get themselves smiling. You can do the same. Your audience will find your smile of enjoyment infectious.

Exhilaration

When preparing your stories, it helps to find a story that excites you—one that was an exciting personal experience for you. When you tell an exciting story, you are charismatic because you're radiating positive energy. Further, your listeners fully engage with the story. Your listeners will enjoy living vicariously through the story you tell.

Challenge

What makes video games so addictive? Two things: the challenge and the visible improvement and reward. Speaker Zig Ziglar once said, "No one would go bowling if they could not see the pins drop."

So, be sure to put something challenging into your preparations. Use this principle that I coined: "Keep score and achieve more." For example, if you have 10 days before an important speech, set up a scoreboard (in your personal journal or on a sheet of paper). Set a goal of 9 minutes of rehearsal for each day. Then set up personal rewards for 27 minutes (3 days) and so forth. Keep track and reward yourself accordingly. By doing this, you will turn rehearsal into a challenging game. The big win comes when your speech blows your audience away.

A final word on challenge: seek to set up ways for you to learn something that keeps you competitive in the marketplace. Challenge yourself to read books or articles to keep up in your particular field.

A person who won't read has no advantage over one who can't read. — Mark Twain

5) Take time for quiet and compassion

As part of my journey as a college instructor of Comparative Religion (for 14 years), I noticed that various spiritual paths have similarities. Some paths encourage one to "pray for others." Other paths suggest that one have quiet time, or meditation, and focus on a positive intention. For example, you can start with the intention of good things for yourself and then you move outward to good intentions for others.

The intentions go in this format:

a) May your happiness increase, [state your own name].
b) May your happiness increase, [name a loved one].
c) May your happiness increase, [name neutral strangers or groups of people].
d) May your happiness increase, [name a person you're having difficulty with].

Sometimes the above is called "a loving-kindness meditation."

Many people report that, after a number of sessions, they experience a new feeling of safety and even connection with all of Creation.

Can you imagine how much you would radiate kindness and compassion after you have practiced this process?

Give it a try, and get the opportunity to experience inner peace.

6) Honor the moment

To be vibrantly alive is to feel it all. Sure, we all feel things. But something strange happens to a number of people when they talk to others. Some put on a frozen fake smile. Others, especially in front of a group, go into "professor mode" and give a lecture instead of simply having a cordial conversation. Unfortunately, these folks do not come across as "real."

To "honor the moment" is to feel the appropriate emotions of what you're talking about—and to let real emotion come out through your face and body language. For example, popular minister Joel Osteen, who regularly addresses capacity crowds of 16,000 or more (not counting his millions of television viewers), has an "open face." He smiles a lot. And when he talks of his father who passed away, you see the real tears come to his eyes. These actions enhance both his Natural Charm Charisma and Warm Trust Charisma.

Recently in my public speaking college class, a student got stuck. "Steve" stood before the audience of students and began the exercise "5 seconds of standing and silence." The exercise called for Steve to communicate with the audience but without words. He could smile, nod, and take a breath as he looked at one student and then another, but he could not speak.

Unfortunately, Steve's facial expression froze, and he nodded at one student after another in a fast progression. He was not honoring the moment. He did not make a personal connection with each student he looked toward.

But this is NOT for you. Take charge of yourself and honor this moment. Seek to discover what an audience member brings to the moment. Employ your Warm Trust Charisma by extending a metaphorical hand in friendship. If the person is truly with you and smiling, return the smile. Don't leave a pasted-on smile on your face. Let a smile naturally flow onto your face and naturally flow off.

If you're talking about something that really shakes you up, then say so: "I have strong feelings about this . . ."

As I've mentioned a few times in this book, "We don't need you to be perfect; we do need you to be genuine."

When people trust a speaker to express her own truth, then they naturally feel a connection with her.

Points to Remember:
- **Darkest Secret #7: People are attracted to those who are vibrantly alive.**
- **Your Countermeasures:**

Use the S.W.I.T.C.H. process:

S – Set up a Switch Phrase
W – Wonder about the "fullness" of the other person
I – Inquire with positivity (ask empowering questions)
T – Take time for quiet and compassion
C – Check out the D.E.C. Advantage
H – Honor the moment

Chapter 9
Expand Your Charisma Power

(This section summarizes some of the techniques I presented earlier. I include this here as a quick reference.)

Would you like to be charismatic, to easily gain cooperation? Here's how: Access your hidden charisma by using the following the Y.O.U process:
Y – Yield to your "Natural Charm Charisma."
O – Open a connection.
U – Unleash your warmth.

1. Yield to your "Natural Charm Charisma"
Some people are naturally good listeners. Others are great storytellers. I guide audiences and clients to enhance these skills. I invite you also to identify your own natural skills and tendencies—or what I call your "Natural Charm Charisma." We don't hear the word charm often these days. *The Merriam-Webster Dictionary* defines *charm* as "compelling attractiveness."

What makes people charming and attractive?
- They listen well.
- They pay attention.
- They make their listener feel like the most important person in the room at that moment.

Do you do any of the above three actions well? If so, be sure to employ them as you meet anyone new.

If you're a natural at telling stories, add two techniques. First, make your story brief. Why? People prefer to talk about themselves. Do not tax their interest. Second, after your story, immediately ask the listener a question. Then the person can offer his or her opinion. People like it better when you listen to them. I advise clients who want to increase their charisma power to be good listeners. When you're listening, you're winning.

Perhaps you consider yourself to be an introvert or simply quiet. That does not need to be a liability. In fact, I've talked with a number of people who have expressed that they don't like presenters who are "too smooth" or "phony" or just plain too loud. They like someone who is a good listener. They say things like "I enjoy interacting with Stephen. He makes me feel comfortable when I'm around him."

Can people say that about you? Do you help people feel comfortable in your presence? If so, great! Keep it up! If not, work on this because it can be a big part of enhancing your Natural Charm Charisma.

Take out a sheet of paper or your personal journal and identify things that you currently do that help a person feel comfortable in your presence.

Recently, I wrote a book, *The Cat Advantage: Catalyze Your Life and Flaunt Your Divine Gifts for Fun, Success and Happiness*. There's a lesson for us about Natural Charm

Charisma in how people view cats. Consider this: We don't ask a cat to be like a dog. Well, at least not if we want good results. What makes cats so attractive? They are completely at ease with their cat nature.

So I'm inviting you to play up your Natural Charm Charisma. That is, I'm inviting you to appreciate what you do naturally to help people feel good in your presence.

2. Open a connection

Charisma encompasses connection. You can make a connection when you talk with one person or with a group of people. One secret of giving an effective speech is to look on the process as a series of one-to-one conversations. Find the friendly faces in your audience and talk with them—one after another.

Have you ever noticed a speaker with his eyes darting around the room? It's distracting, and it makes him look nervous. Here's a solution: Practice giving a paragraph to a person. Look at one person and give that individual around four sentences. Give them a whole idea with a couple of supporting sentences. When you're ready to cover the next idea, move to a different person for that paragraph.

Can you see how focusing on one person for about eight seconds opens a connection with that individual?

Here's another technique for connecting with someone: Ask a question and listen. Then say back what you heard so that the person knows you really heard them. I'm not talking about "parroting back" what the person said. Instead, you look the person in the eyes and show how you care and how you find what they said to be important. You can even say something like: "Andy, I hear that you want Process 1-A to stay in the mix. I'm with you on that. It is important to . . ."

Use the above methods, and make that connection.

3. Unleash your warmth

Charisma is more than being smooth or magnetic. It's about being warm and being trusted.

How do you let your warmth come through? By preparing and rehearsing days ahead of time.

The top professionals in the world know the value of practice. Olympic athletes train constantly until something that was awkward becomes something they do with ease and grace. Music headliners rehearse their singing and dancing hundreds of times so that on stage their moves look effortless. Actors immerse themselves in their roles 24/7 so that they truly become that character. For instance, in preparing for his role as the Terminator, Arnold Schwarzenegger kept a shotgun next to his desk so that at every spare moment he could practice his one-handed cock-the-gun movements because he knew that his character, a machine, would move with precision and economy.

So to be a professional who comes across as naturally warm, you must practice and rehearse! But practice and rehearse what? For one thing, your opening comments and closing comments for conversations you'll have with strangers.

You may say, "But that sounds so cold and calculating. How can that possibly unleash my 'warmth'?" Rehearsal helps you avoid being so nervous that your body language becomes distracting. Instead, you'll come across as warm because you'll know what to do and you will have practiced ahead of time.

Here are some examples of opening comments for beginning a new conversation:
- "Hello. How do you know Mark, our host?"
- "Hi. How is the conference going for you?"
- "Hello. I'm curious. What do you like most about

this association?"

By using these easy-question openings, you will get the other person talking, which almost always creates a warm connection.

Now, let's talk about closing a conversation, which can in some cases be much stickier, making the need for practice even more important. Here are two techniques you can use:

- You say, "Oh, it's been great talking with you. I promised my supervisor that I'd mingle. It would be great to stay in contact with you. Do you have a card?" [They give you a business card].
- If they do not have a business card, you pull out one of your cards and say, "Oh, that's fine. I'll make you one. Are you at gmail or yahoo?" [Then you write down their email address.]

Remember, charisma is really about making a connection. It's not about being flashy. Instead, focus on unleashing your Natural Charm Charisma. Let other people enjoy being with you.

Chapter 10
Develop Your Personal Leverage

Have you ever felt like you were in presence of a powerful person? They had some form of charisma—yes?

Often that person has special knowledge. Plus, the person "knows that they know." This is part of something called "metacognition," which is thinking about your thinking. To know that you know special knowledge gives you an advantage: You actually have true power afforded you by that special knowledge. And then you naturally radiate strength.

Imagine that you knew that you truly had power. In this case, we're talking about a certain form of power: Leverage. Often, leverage is about expending little effort for a big, positive result.

Recently, in viewing the current global recession, I had the idea of writing a book that would help people take care of themselves and their families. Such a book would provide ways to increase one's leverage and power. Now, such knowledge is useful to anyone who wants to radiate charisma. The following techniques can help you increase your personal leverage, so we'll use the term L.E.V.E.R.

Here is the L.E.V.E.R. process:

L – Let the customer "win"
E – Eliminate unnecessary routines
V – Verify multiple streams of income
E – Engage in speedy delivery
R – Regularly pivot fast

The following examples relate to business. Why? Much of the time we're meeting new people in course of our business day.

1. Let the customer "win"

When I say "win," I'm talking about two things. First, you want the customer to feel that he or she has come out well in any transaction. In essence, the customer is already truly winning by receiving excellent service or a valuable product. But I'm also talking about giving the customer a "bonus." Let them feel that they "beat you."

This may feel like a counterintuitive way to radiate charisma. But the truth is: In the current recession, competition is fierce. Not only are you going up against your standard competitors for business, but you're also competing against your customers' internal hesitation and fear. In hard times, people are less likely to spend money.

What would overcome such fear? A huge bargain. For example, a friend recently took an online course related to the Law of Attraction. The originator of the course advertised that the course fee was normally $500, but with this one-time special offer, you could get that course for only $17.00! Yes, you read that right.

Guess what happened? Anyone who got the course at only $17.00 felt like he or she won!

Ultimately, it is the originator of such a course who wins. If an offer like this is sent out to 60,000 people and 2% purchase the product, the originator gains a gross income of $20,400.

Some potential customers might say, "This is too good to be true." However, here are two factors that would reduce the possibility of that conclusion. To get a substantial number of sales, the originator of the course needs to do a couple of things:

1) Prove that this is a special one-time offer that is only available to people on this special, exclusive list, and
2) Have a track record of successfully serving subscribers and clients.

From the above, do you see the power of "letting the customer 'win'"? How can you apply this insight to your own work life?

2. Eliminate unnecessary routines

Years ago, my team members had to package and send my books to 15 countries. Such activity kept us away from doing other things. Back then, we wrote it off as the "cost of opportunity." Now, I have Amazon.com do all the shipping. In essence, I eliminated the shipping routine from our workdays.

Look at your own business to consider how you can outsource some routine work. Focus your time on what only you can do. My personal time is better spent in creating products, not shipping them.

3. Verify multiple streams of income

Ideally, you make money every day with something that does not involve your personal time or efforts. For example, a number of my colleagues make money with eBooks created for Amazon Kindle. They do the work once (writing the book) and they get paid over and over again. This is one of their streams of income.

Let's go back to the ideas of leverage, power, and charisma. If all of your money comes from only one source, it's likely that you may be scared that the source will dry up. And it's a legitimate concern. For instance, I know a software engineer "Henry" who moved across the country to start a new job. Within months, the situation changed, and the job was gone. Now Henry is scrambling for another job, and his desperation is showing. If Henry had arranged to make money in a number of ways, total desperation would leave his thoughts and feelings, and he would be in a much better position to find additional employment.

How can you create multiple sources of income?

4. Engage in speedy delivery

Simply put, to compete in today's marketplace, you must provide goods and services quickly. We're all on the Internet, and we get upset if there's a downloading delay of a mere 10 seconds. Now, multiply that easily-frustrated state of mind by, let's say ten, and you get an idea of how people feel about their work lives. We want relief, and we want it now!

Amazon.com and iTunes provide music downloads in less than a minute. Many of us are used to this speed of delivery. Technology has now provided instant downloading of digital products. It's time for a person who wants leverage and power to seriously consider how to make instant downloads of digital products part of their income stream.

Is there something that you know that someone may want to learn from you? Then you have the makings of a potential digital product. Now, with services like ejunkie.com, you can put up some form of product for instant download.

5. Regularly pivot fast

The person with more options and the will to make tough decisions has an advantage in business and even personal relationships. "Pivoting fast" can be about protecting yourself from a bad situation.

Here's an example of pivoting fast to protect yourself from losing money. One of my clients noticed that she was not getting enough clients through her website. Her shopping cart sales were non-existent. Many people in her position would just "let it ride." Not my client. She called up her shopping cart service and asked about lower cost versions of the shopping cart service. She learned that she could put the shopping cart service on a six-month hiatus. Instantly, she saved hundreds of dollars in monthly fees.

Now, she had time to figure her next strategy. Was she going to invest effort (and perhaps, money) in increasing the traffic to her website? Would she start a blog instead? Or would she concentrate on having BarnesandNoble.com and Amazon.com sell her products? By pivoting fast, she gave herself the leeway she needed to redirect her business.

This ability to pivot fast is one strength of a small business. The business owner can make a quick and appropriate decision and jump into a new segment of the marketplace. So pivoting fast can be about jumping into an opportunity.

For example, after I saw how well my book *Darkest Secrets*

of Persuasion and Seduction Masters: How to Protect Yourself and Turn the Power to Good did on Amazon.com, I immediately hired contractors to assist me with editing another book with a similar theme: *Darkest Secrets of Negotiation Masters.*

Then I took that theme and turned it into an entire series:
- Darkest Secrets of Business Communication
- Darkest Secrets of the Film and Television Industry Every Actor Should Know
- Darkest Secrets of Spiritual Seduction Masters
- Darkest Secrets of Small Business Marketing
- Darkest Secrets of the Film and Television Industry Every Actor Should Know
- Darkest Secrets of Film Directing
- Darkest Secrets of Making a Pitch to the Film and Television Industry

Now you get the idea about how to group a bunch of topics under one brand, such as the "Darkest Secrets of."

To increase your personal leverage, stay observant. See how the marketplace has changed. And decide how you can pivot and get into action.

Also, observe where your business may be leaking money, then pivot fast and plug the hole!

* * *

Charisma often rests on true power and leverage. Use the above five methods to increase your leverage and then you'll naturally radiate a quiet power.

Book II
How to Be a Charismatic Leader

When are you a leader? Some of us are leaders in our job—perhaps, as a team lead, manager, or even CEO. However, all of us lead at some point. You lead a friend to see a movie you want to see together. You lead a family member to consider a particular purchase. You lead co-workers to support a suggestion you made for a work process.

To enhance your charisma in this area, use the L.E.A.D.S. process:

L – Listen
E – Engage their emotions
A – Act
D – Delegate
S – Study leadership

1. Listen

The leader needs to get a person to "buy in" to the project or the next step. One essential method of leadership is to listen to the team member's ideas. This does not necessarily mean you approve of the person's ideas or suggestions, but you set a comfortable atmosphere in which people can voice their opinions.

For example, when someone joins my team working on my graphic novel *TimePulse*, I share my approach to the work:

"I want to hear your ideas. Often, I'll say, 'Sounds good. Do that.' Sometimes, I may not be able to incorporate the idea because I'm thinking of the whole saga—all three graphic novels in the trilogy. But there are times when a new idea results in a new character or twist in the story. I'm inspired by how Walt Disney would get his team members to improve the projects. In the middle of developing an animated film, he would go to the team and say, 'Plus this.' That is, improve it and add to it."

Then, with a smile, I conclude: "This 'plus this' process is how we work collaboratively here."

How do you create an opportunity in which you listen to team members' ideas? You ask effective questions like:
- "Anything else I need to know?"
- "Do you have any questions?"
- "How would you improve this?"
- "What is your recommendation?"
- "How is the process going for you so far?"

Realize that people more readily follow when they know that their leader listens, cares, and has the wisdom to make a project better by incorporating the skills and talents of all involved.

2. Engage their emotions

Positive emotions provide energy to get things done. On the other hand, negative emotions may function as distractions or blocks to productivity. You, as the leader, can make choices so that more often people are energized to be productive. What kind of choices? The ones that support your team members' positive emotions.

Unfortunately, I have frequently heard friends complain about their managers. Somewhere during the conversation, it becomes clear to me that their managers simply have not availed themselves of training in leadership best practices.

Speaking of best practices, here is a brief summary of actions by effective leaders and the results they inspire:

a) Listen—which inspires loyalty and trust
b) Remain calm in the face of trouble—which inspires trust
c) Offer praise—which inspires positive, energizing emotion
d) Act in decisive ways—which inspires trust and compliance
e) Envision excellent results—which inspires enthusiasm and, often, exhilaration.

These above five actions are positive ways to engage team members' emotions. Author/researcher Daniel Goleman notes that successful leaders have empathy, which includes "the ability to understand the emotional makeup of other people." He also wrote that successful leaders have "skill in treating people according to their emotional reactions."

Find ways to incorporate the above five practices into your leadership.

3. Act

To be an effective leader, you need to "lead from the front." This means that you're visible on the metaphorical battlefield, there to assist and encourage. One way I do that is to make myself available to team members when they're working on projects. For example, my team members (who work in various locations) can reach me by phone, email and chat, and I respond quickly.

Often, I have heard friends frustrated with their bosses who are not available to provide essential feedback. It seems that the bosses have stepped away with their own families for time off, while their subordinates have to stay at work, toiling during the weekend to meet some deadline.

Although I support a leader devoting time to family and self-renewal, I also feel that a wise leader is available to his or her "troops" when they are working.

Your soldiers are watching. They need to see you and hear you, so act like you care. Act like you're on the same team. Act like a leader.

4. Delegate

Effective leaders know that they can't do everything themselves. That's why they must gain skills in delegation. The goal is to bring out the best performance in their team members.

Here are two important methods of delegation:
a) Avoid hovering by creating "natural check-in points."
b) Use "completed staff work." (I provide an explanation below.)

a) Avoid hovering by creating "natural check-in points."

An ineffective leader micromanages the time and efforts of his subordinates. He hovers over his workers as if looking for a mistake. Naturally, people resent that. After all, they're adults, and they bring their own ways of working to a project. Hovering also torpedoes a leader's charisma. For one thing, it makes him look overly concerned and even afraid. That is NOT the energy of a charismatic leader.

So don't hover over a team member. Instead, create "natural check-in points." That is, begin by asking the team member something like, "When do you think you'll have a rough draft of that graphic?" You integrate the team member's answers with setting up a schedule of checking in with her progress. Make sure that the team member knows that you see your job as making sure that she has what she needs (resources and your direction) to do a great job. The natural check-in point is for you to learn about how things are going. Many of us have heard the phrase: "You get what you inspect, not what you expect." So checking in remains a primary part of your job as the leader. However, you also need to demonstrate appropriate confidence that your skilled team member can make progress. By checking in and setting a schedule, you'll know the status of the work.

b) Use "completed staff work."

It's reported that Napoleon led with efficiency. How? He succeeded in getting his generals to think through problems before bringing them to him. He said something like: "If you see a problem, before you come to me, I want you to come up with three solutions, endorse one, and then tell me your reasons for endorsing that one solution."

The above methodology is called "completed staff work."

I use it frequently. For example, I invite the artists for my TimePulse graphic novel to unleash their creativity. I have them draw three quick sketches (called thumbnail sketches) of a portion of a page and then choose their favorite version of an image. I ask them to endorse one version and inform me of their reasoning.

I learn a lot from my artists this way and often say, "Sounds good. I like your reasons. We'll go with the version you recommended."

5. Study leadership

How do you become proficient in a field? Study. I study every day, reading books on leadership, communication, and the various other fields I keep up with. I tend to read 74 books per year. Every year, I attend workshops to improve my communication, coaching and leadership skills.

Realize that a great deal of leadership comes down to both will and learnable skills. You must begin with the will and desire to become an effective leader. From there you take the willful energy and apply it to your study efforts.

Why is it important to study so much? That way, when you have a troublesome situation, you have a number of options in mind because you have read about techniques and case studies.

In addition, you may need to "unlearn" detrimental behaviors. Many leaders have developed bad habits that undermine good leadership. They have to identify these tendencies and compensate for them.

If a leader has a disruptive tendency, such as being abrupt, he can use willpower to suppress that tendency. For example, "John" has learned that he tends to be abrupt, but he has resolved to try to curb his rude behaviors for an upcoming meeting. It's best that John schedule the meeting at a time when he feels strong. Since John knows that his willpower tends to fade over the course of the day, he schedules the meeting in the morning. Now John will have the energy to restrain his natural tendency to cut people off and not hear them out. He'll be able to pause and listen better and longer.

How did I learn of the above topics of willpower, leadership, and communication? I studied recent books highlighting research on those subjects. Now I'm inviting you to study leadership. Make it a lifelong endeavor that will improve your work life.

Book III
Influence People with Your Words

How often do you need to influence someone in your daily life? If you said, "only a couple of times a day," you may not have included all of the times when you just want people to stay neutral. Our words can move a person to cooperation or resistance. In order to be more skillful in our verbal expression, use the W.O.R.D. process:

W – Work in "you" and "we"

O – Open with a benefit

R – Reveal stories

D – Direct the conversation through your questions—and listen up

1. Work in "you" and "we"

One of my mentors taught me an essential practice for public speaking: Speak in terms of "you" and "we." When you say "I want," you're often losing the audience. Why? People are preoccupied with their own problems. They're thinking things like: "Who cares what you want? I've got real problems here, and you're not helping me. You're just wasting my time!"

But when you talk about methods that will "help you," the audience focuses on your words just as a matter of self-interest.

Then, you can use another key word to get the audience to feel like you're one of them. That word is we. Say we as in "We often face situations in which . . ."

When you give people information that they find useful, you do something important. Plus, you avoid bringing up needless resistance. The truth is: People tend to naturally resist new ideas. So you're going to get at least some "natural resistance." Your task is to avoid needless resistance that can take the form of subconscious thoughts like: "You're talking about what you want. You don't care about me and what I'm facing."

In my public speaking classes, I often say, "To influence people, minimize resistance."

Talking about your desires merely intensifies other people's resistance. Instead, talk in terms of how you care that they get what they want.

2. Open with a benefit

What seizes people's attention? Talking about something that will improve their lives.

Mention the benefits of your speech in the introduction. For example, during a presentation once, I said, "If I could share with you four things that Ross Perot* did that made him a billionaire in eight years, would that be helpful to you? Would you be interested?"

It was an interested audience, so they replied with: "Yes!" and "Hell, yes!"

Since I brought up the topic: I'll say that Ross Perot had 1) technology that he could bring to each state in turn, 2) motivated sales people who enjoyed stock options, 3) persistence and 4) an initial public offering. (I go into detail in my book Year of Awesome!*)*

When listeners hear you talk, three questions arise, at least in their subconscious mind. I call these the 3 W's:
- "Who are you?"
- "Why should I listen to you?"
- "What's in it for me?"

When you start by talking about the benefits for your listeners, you have zeroed in on that last, and probably most important, W—the "what's in it for me?" question.

You can even use this technique in less formal communications. For instance, you can influence people in your emails by highlighting benefits. You could write something like: "George, here's how implementing Process X-1 will lighten your workload."

Ineffective people talk about how they want something. They assume that their listeners will be spellbound if they talk about how some new procedure will benefit the company you both work for. Let's face facts. Modern life is tough, and people are hoping to find something that will bring ease into their own lives. If you want to be effective, then show them how they can personally benefit from what you're talking about.

What are some personal benefits you can focus on?
- a procedure that lightens their workload.
- a technique that saves their time.
- a method that takes the stress out of an interaction.
- a process that makes them look good to their supervisor, which can help them earn a raise.

A person's priorities can be summed up in this request: "Reduce my stress, help me protect my job, help me get more money, and I'll listen to you."

3. Reveal stories

What makes a good story? Cognitive scientist George Lakoff writes about how human beings are conditioned to expect certain elements in a story: the hero, the helper, the villain, and the victim. If you give people the above elements, they find it easy to understand your story. Further, they will feel connected to you and your story.

Often, a smart salesperson will position herself as the helper. Using her comments skillfully, the salesperson guides the buyer to feel like a hero in making the purchasing decision.

Another way to seize the listener's attention is to use a meme or two in your story. A meme is often described as an "idea virus." For example, some years ago, numerous people felt that a certain president of the United States had not acted quickly enough to relieve the suffering of thousands of people in the aftermath of a disaster. Members of that president's political party said, "Now is not the time for finger pointing." Over and over again these politicians repeated that phrase until it became an "idea virus" that went from person to person.

Author Richard Brodie identified the following types of memes. There may be other memes, but I find this list quite useful for understanding how communication works:

1. Evangelism
2. Elitism
3. Fear of punishment
4. Crisis
5. Tradition

6. Low Risk, High Reward

Here's an example of a phrase a salesperson might use in the middle of a conversation. ". . . then you can save money and protect your job." The salesperson touches on the meme, Fear of punishment.

What does the salesperson accomplish with touching on memes? She has reached the customer on a deeper level. And she is more likely to get the sale.

Another powerful technique is: Tell a story from the point of view of a satisfied customer. This is often referred to as a "third-party endorsement." That is, a third person—not the salesperson or the potential buyer—provides a credible recommendation.

Finally, I'll share these elements of a good story:
- intense problem
- tension and suspense
- triumphant ending

Your job is to inspire both interest and suspense. When you do this, the listener will hang on your words, waiting to hear how things turned out.

In this way, your words will be influential.

4. Direct the conversation through your questions—and listen up

How are things going for you?

Did your thoughts just go to something that happened early today? You can see how powerful questions are. They guide the thinking of the listener.

Who leads a conversation? The one who asks the questions.

But make your questions easy to answer. Avoid putting

people on the spot. And word your questions carefully.

For example, even the question, "How are things going for you?" is, for many people, less confrontational than the usual "How are you doing?" If someone is in a low mood, he may blame himself for feeling out of sorts. But when you say, "How are things going for you?" that places the responsibility outside the person and upon "the things."

Researchers also note that many men feel a subtle undercurrent of competition. Author John Gray notes that if a woman asks a man, "Can you get that item for me?" it feels confrontational. It's like she's asking, "Do you have the capacity to get the item?"

Gray suggests that the question be formed as "Would you get that item for me?" There is no hint of aspersion about ability. Now, it is about whether the man wants to or decides to be helpful. This type of question supports the man's autonomy—or some might say—his ego.

Asking questions that support autonomy is valuable for conversations with people of either gender. This is the reason that I invite you to ask, when possible, easy and gentle questions. People feel good as they answer a question that's easy to answer.

The master technique consists of pre-planning your questions. You want to guide your listeners along the path that you want them to experience. You want them to experience certain feelings and draw particular conclusions. How do you do that? You bring up your pre-planned topics via the questions you pose to the listeners.

Be sure to listen well to their answers. Listening well shows how you value them. They will feel a real connection with you.

Here are the "Do's" of good listening:
- Do lean forward a bit to show, through body

language, that you're listening.
- Do make appropriate eye contact.
- Do respond by confirming that you heard what they said.

Reply with something like: "I heard you say that coming in on budget is important to you."

Here are the "Don'ts" of good listening:
- Don't interrupt.
- Don't let your eyes wander around the room.
- Don't make light of the person's concerns.

Even if you know that something else is more important to the success of a project, avoid minimizing the other person's concerns.

Affirm the importance of the person's feelings and observations. You could say something like: "I can hear how Step 1 is important to you. You feel that people will become confused if they do not learn the clearing process. Do I have that about right?"

A good listener verifies that he or she understands the speaker's position. Hence you use the question: "Do I have that about right?"

Asking good questions and listening well help you assure the other person that she is worthwhile to you.

Everyone has an invisible sign hanging from their neck saying, 'Make me feel important.' Never forget this message when working with people. — Mary Kay Ash

* * *

Be careful with your words. Some authors cite an old

phrase that words are only 7% of your communication and the rest is comprised of tone and body language. That may or may not be true. But if you use clumsy words, the 7% of what you do say can destroy your communication.

Follow these guidelines to make your words influential:

W – Work in "you" and "we"
O – Open with a benefit
R – Reveal stories
D – Direct the conversation through your questions—and listen up

Book IV
Charisma for Introverts

Get People to Feel Your Charisma and Be Influenced by Your Words

Want to feel confident? Do you want people to feel your charisma and be influenced by your words? Here's how: use the S.H.I.N.E. process:

S – Start inside (your personal brand)
H – Highlight your bright moments
I – Ignite rehearsal
N – Neutralize mixed feelings
E – Energize yourself

In this section, I'll be addressing some insights that demonstrate that one can be an introvert and still express charisma.

If you're an extrovert, you can employ these methods, too.

1. Start inside (your personal brand)
Perhaps, you've heard: "She's comfortable in her own

skin." One way to feel that level of comfort is to do a bit of self-reflection on your personal brand. Why? Because you have a reputation (also known as a personal brand) whether you take action to control it or not. In a nutshell, your personal brand is your answer to the question: "What are you best known for?"

Here are some examples that my clients use for describing themselves:

- "I'm best known for finding low-cost solutions to tough problems."
- "I'm best known for connecting with the audience on the heart level."

When you know your personal brand, then you can shine. Why? Because when you talk with someone, you'll be clear in your communication.

Further, identify what about your personal brand makes you glad to get up in the morning. One of my editors asked, "What if your personal brand does not make you glad?" I replied, "Then, the personal brand is off. A top flight, effective personal brand is aligned with your best self." For example, just before this writing, I was interviewed on a radio show. When I talked about how I help people to be emotionally strong and make dreams come true, I was in complete alignment with my personal brand because it makes me glad to help my clients and students in this way.

How are you helping others? Make that part of your personal brand.

Your first task is to reflect and become aware of your true personal brand—one that aligns with your heart.

The next task is to prepare to effectively communicate your personal brand. A number of introverts say, "I'm good talking with people one-to-one, but talking to a group is a big problem for me." If you're called to give a presentation, use this useful method: Have a series of one-to-one conversations. By this I mean, address your presentation to one person in the audience and then address another person some distance away from that person. In this way, it looks like you're speaking to a number of people in the audience.

First, greet audience members and talk with them before your presentation. Ask them a couple of questions and make a connection. Then, when you give your presentation, talk to the friendly faces in the group. When you speak, give a whole paragraph to one person. By this I mean to present a whole idea with a couple of sentences supporting your idea. Then move on to another friendly face. In this way, you do have a series of one-to-one conversations.

2. Highlight your bright moments

Sometimes when I help a client hone her speech (or a pitch for her product), I ask, "What part of this topic or what story do you want to share? What are you happy about?" By asking these questions, I'm guiding her to tap into her positive energy. To be charismatic, you need to do the same. Start from an authentic place inside yourself.

What is an authentic place inside yourself? It's where you feel "full" and not empty. It's a place where you're doing something because it feels aligned with who you are. It is NOT the mere focus on trying to get approval. This authentic place is where you feel good about what you do. The good feelings that you have about what you do are what I call "your bright moments." For example, I enjoy inspiring laughter in my audience. And they can see my enjoyment on my face. Similarly, I invite you to make visible to your audience those elements of what you enjoy doing. Get clear in your own mind about them and then highlight them for your audience.

3. Ignite rehearsal

I share with my public speaking college students, "Anytime you feel fearful, rehearse." That's the essence of quieting down any fear you may feel. The more you rehearse, the better you get—and the more you know that you are getting better. Knowing that you really know the material gives you that assurance you crave.

You need to say your words and practice out loud. It's not enough for you to merely read over your notes. You need to feel whether the words flow well coming out of your mouth. You can rehearse by calling a friend and saying, "Do you have a minute so that I can practice the opening of my speech?" You can then move on to another friend to practice the middle or the closing of your speech. Late at night, you can call your own phone answering system and rehearse by recording your spoken words.

4. Neutralize mixed feelings

Many of us get thwarted by mixed feelings. Some of our feelings may be inspired by negative comments from parents and guardians such as: "Who do you think you are? You aren't that smart." and "You're not that [pretty, good at this—or something else]."

Perhaps these elders were trying to prevent us from "getting a big head" or "becoming arrogant." Maybe they didn't realize that there's a big difference between arrogance and quietly knowing that you have achieved competence.

My point here is this: charismatic people look confident because they know that they're good at something. They do not apologize for it. They worked hard to become proficient at what they do. They know that they work hard to provide their clients with great service. And the clients pick up on the confident person's inner knowing that he or she is quite capable. Think about it: Do you want to hire a confident surgeon or a tentative one?

The way to neutralize mixed feelings is to take action so that you live up to your personal brand. My clients study hard and rehearse. They do the work to make sure that they are on their toes for each presentation. Rehearsal works.

5. Energize yourself

Here's where knowing that you're an introvert can give you an edge. To be charismatic, you need lots of energy. You simply must radiate the energy of calmness and confidence. However, unlike an extrovert, who finds it invigorating to be around a lot of people, an introvert recharges by getting some time alone.

Observing that I have some introvert tendencies, I take regular downtime or quiet time each day, during which I'm away from everyone, including family members. I find this essential so that I have an abundance of energy for family, audiences, and my graduate students and clients.

One of the reasons that I wanted to write this section is that I want to relieve introverts of the guilt that they may feel. Some may feel that they do not go to enough networking events. Others may feel guilty when they try to get some alone-time away from family. The truth that I've discovered for myself is that I simply feel better when I schedule daily alone time. If you're an introvert, schedule alone time for recharging; this is something that you do for yourself and for those around you. A miserable introvert does no one any good.

Instead, take care of yourself and recharge your energy. You'll be better at expressing your natural charm and charisma.

Book Four – continued

Flex Your Charisma in Media—for Introverts

A smile can start a cascade of kindness. — Tom Marcoux

Some introverts tell me that they dread having to deal with the media to publicize their business. They say, "I'm a quiet person. I don't like being pushy with anyone."

In this section, we'll dispel the myth that you need to be pushy. In addition, you'll learn how to prepare so that you're more at ease. You'll be able to interact with a journalist in a comfortable way, which can raise your own smile and then perhaps, inspire him to smile as well. When the journalist feels respected, particularly if his time is respected, he feels better about you and the material that you provide in a press release. You want the media person to feel good and to be kind to you both: He gets a valuable story, and you get valuable publicity.

To get your story in a magazine or newspaper or to be a guest on someone's blog, you do NOT need to push yourself. Instead of expending a big effort, you can do simple things to make a warm connection with the media person.

You can use your Natural Charm Charisma as an introvert. I know this personally: In getting exposure on TV, radio, magazines, newspapers, and other people's blogs, I have not had to be "salesman-like" or pushy. Instead, I was straight-to-the point, friendly, and positive.

Now, how can you access your Natural Charm Charisma? If you're an introvert, tune into what you do naturally. Many introverts mention these tendencies:
1) They like to do research on their own.
2) They like to think through their answers before having people pose questions.
3) They prefer to talk one-on-one with an individual.
4) They recover their energy by recharging while they're alone.

The short answer for pitching well to the media is to utilize your tendencies and learn to get obstacles out of the way. And then you'll make a warm connection.

Here are methods to make a warm connection that form the M.E.D.I.A. process:
M – Make it about them
E – Entertain
D – Describe it quickly (personal brand and "key words")
I – Inquire (ask and do research)
A – Assign yourself a rehearsal schedule

1. Make it about them

Media people (journalists, bloggers, TV show guest schedulers) face crushing deadlines all of the time. They're busy! And they hate it when someone appears to waste their time. So you must come up with a script of what you'll say

to the person and rehearse it so that you can quickly and clearly communicate:
- Who you are
- What your story is
- How their audience will benefit

Here's an example:

"Hello, Ms. Smythe. I'm George Javen, President of Javen Enterprises. I've got a story that will provide your readers with ways to save one hour a day and line themselves up for a raise. Would you like me to email or fax the press release?"

Fit your approach to the needs of the journalist and the desires of his or her target audience. How? Read articles published by the journalist or watch/listen to episodes of the person's TV/radio show. Identify how the viewers or readers respond. With blogs, you have an easier time because you can see how many Facebook shares and comments are posted. With TV/radio, you can discover how often certain topics are booked on a particular show.

2. Entertain

When I say "entertain," I do not mean that you must become a standup comedian and necessarily get the journalist to laugh when he answers your phone call. But it does help to first make sure that your message is concise.

Cinema is life with the boring parts cut out.
— Alfred Hitchcock

As a filmmaker, I like Hitchcock's quote. It also reminds me to make my pitch to a journalist interesting—and if possible entertaining. I must also be ready to respond to any on-the-spot questions that the journalist may ask with my best, most interesting story (or stories) and details. Let me illustrate.

Let's say I'm pitching a story about my book on time management. I would include a comment from an audience member Jaclyn Freitas: "Using Tom's methods, I got more done in two weeks than in six months." [The methods she references and more are in my book, *Soar! Nothing Can Stop You This Year*. Look inside the book at Amazon.com.]

The journalist might respond: "What methods?" Then, I'd go into detail about my methods that overcome procrastination and eliminate time-wasters.

Another part of "entertain" can be to briefly praise the journalist and express something you observed. How does this entertain? To put it simply, it just makes them feel good. Many people just press on during their workday. Anything that reminds them of some "good news" (how they did well) will brighten their day.

Here is an example:

Late in a conversation with "Joe," a journalist, I say, "Thanks, Joe, for being willing to take a look at my press release. I'll get that in an email to you within five minutes. By the way, I read your blog post about eliminating unnecessary meetings. I saw the many grateful comments. I remember SarahCrewAZ saying, 'You just saved four years of my life!'"

Joe responds with a chuckle, "Yeah, that's my most popular post ever!"

In this situation, Joe felt praised and noticed. That creates a neural association of good thoughts and feelings to you and whatever is in your press release. It may be a stretch to say that Joe was "entertained," but we can assume that he probably felt good and that he would likely be predisposed to cooperate with the person seeking publicity.

3. Describe it quickly (personal brand and "key words")

Many introverts say that they're good when talking one-on-one with people, but they have trouble with "thinking on their feet." They mean that being spontaneous with their replies can be tough. Some of them comment: "I need time to think. I don't want to throw out any random thought."

Introverts can alleviate this concern by getting prepared before calling a media person. For instance, you can have all your notes spread out on the table in front of you. You can take your time before the call to write up these notes and figure out what you're going to say. And as you develop your pitch for your story, you need to remember to say it with few words. (That's why I titled this section "describe the topic quickly.") Again, we must realize that the media person is extremely busy.

One way to shape your pitch is to include a mention of your personal brand. Remember, your personal brand is your answer to the question: "What are you best known for?"

Here are some examples:

Clinical Psychologist with a new book to promote: "I'm best known for helping children thrive after they've survived trauma."

Bakery Owner: "I'm best known for my cupcakes that children find delicious and mothers find full of healthy nutrition."

Finally, identify what you might call your "key words." Think about the benefits that the media person's audience wants. Then use those benefits as key words in your pitch to the journalist.

Use phrases like these:
- ". . . helps your viewers increase their productivity by 37 percent."
- ". . . gets your blog readers excited about how they'll be able to do . . ."

4. Inquire (ask and do research)

Start by jotting down on a sheet of paper: "What are 10 questions I do NOT want to answer?" Then list such questions. This list helps you prepare for the tough questions that you may be asked. After generating the list, write down two answers for each question. Now, you have 20 answers for potential curve balls thrown your way, and you're much better prepared than most people called upon to give any sort of presentation.

Many introverts report that they like doing research and looking up things when they are alone. Use that personal preference (if you have it), and thoroughly prepare before you call anyone in the media.

5. Assign yourself a rehearsal schedule

Recently, before a radio host interviewed me on the topic of "Be Emotionally Strong and Make Dreams Come True," I lined up three top professionals I know to do "mock interviews" with me. As friends of mine, these three wanted to help me, but they're really busy. So I asked only for a few minutes of their listening time. I also rehearsed with a family member before calling them back for my appointments.

After working with these three "interviewers," my confidence about being prepared grew because I could feel and experience how prepared I was.

This next method related to rehearsal is so valuable that I share it often (even another time in this book). Set up a schedule of rehearsing 9 minutes a day for several days before you contact a media person. Why? For one thing, 9 minutes per day is a totally doable number for even the busiest of people. In addition, even though it is a small amount of time, your subconscious mind will continue to work on your pitch for the rest of the day. Don't forget to set up a reward that you give yourself for having those rehearsal sessions.

Keep a log of your progress. A number of introverts talk about how they like to do research, that they want the facts. So keep up with your own facts and prove to yourself that you have done excellent work to prepare yourself to talk with a media person. Use this principle: Keep score and achieve more.

Use the above techniques when it comes to your rehearsal, and you will not only build up your own confidence but also your charisma. Do what you need to do to build yourself up so that you're ready for any encounter with a media person.

Book V
Remove Blocks to Happiness and Your Charisma Radiates Naturally

Do you know someone who radiates positive energy? Do you like to be near that person? I imagine so.

On the other hand, many of us know someone who seems be a bottomless pit of complaining and misery. This person probably never learned to bolster his or her own happiness.

But this is NOT for you. This section is about removing blocks to happiness so that you can radiate charisma naturally.

Create Lots of Personal Energy to Make Your Dreams Come True

To make your dreams come true, you need lots of personal energy. This means you need to make a choice. Will you choose to find ways to empower yourself? If so, this requires change.

We generally change ourselves for one of two reasons: inspiration or desperation. — *Jim Rohn*

The problem with changing out of desperation is that is it drains our energy. So instead, we're going to look at ways to fill you up with positive energy and uplifting thoughts and feelings.

Start thinking of positive moments and even experiencing happy moments each day.

We don't remember days, we remember moments. — Cesare Pavese

To get to those positive moments, we need to become skillful in removing blocks to our happiness. Here are five such blocks:

F – Fear
E – Expectations
A – Approval
R – Resistance (judgment)
S – Source of identity

You probably noticed that the 5 blocks form the word F.E.A.R.S.

It turns out that all 5 blocks not only torpedo our happiness, but they also derail our success.

We'll talk about these elements in turn.

1. Fear

Here are three techniques that reduce fear:
a) Reduce the downside
b) Preset your safety net
c) Use fear to jumpstart your preparation.

a) Reduce the downside

You can get yourself into action if you minimize your exposure to harsh outcomes. For example, let's say you'd like to write a book. You don't know what title would be appropriate or meet with readers' approval. First, you could try out the title on a blog article that you wrote. In that way, you have not risked any money. Later, if you receive a lot of positive response to the blog article, you might consider using that title for a small book. In this way, you keep the downside small.

b) Preset your safety net
As a writer, I preset my safety net by hiring two editors for each book I write. Now it's your turn: Consider getting some coaching. Have experts watch your back.

c) Use fear to jumpstart your preparation
Audience members tell me that they remember my phrase: "Courage is easier when I'm prepared." Any time you feel fear, find ways to rehearse or get expert advice for improving your speech or project.

It is important for you to quiet down fear so that you can take action. The successful people I have interviewed for books and articles have a particular characteristic: They do not wait to feel comfortable and to be totally free of fear before they take action. They consistently put lots of effort into rehearsal and preparation. For example, Steve Jobs put hundreds of hours into his big product launch presentations. When he launched the iPhone at MacWorld in 2007, he looked relaxed and spontaneous, but his team members reported that his speech was painstakingly prepared.

Power Question: How can you prepare and rehearse—and therefore reduce any associated fear?

2. Expectations
Expectations can drain your energy and cripple your productivity. Worse—they can make you plain miserable. I

have a friend who was stuck in a job and living situation for 10 years. He kept complaining to me how it was unfair for him to be slammed by troublesome things in life. In fact, he was angry that God had allowed unfair things to happen to him. You see, he had big expectations, and life was not going his way.

All of this anger and complaining prevented him from seeing opportunities. He was too busy talking about what he did not get or what had been taken away to see all the blessings and opportunities in his life.

To make your dreams come true, you need to be like a clear window. Anger, expectations, and complaining are like dust clouding up a window. You can't see your way forward.

Instead, turn your expectations into mere preferences. What does that mean? It means that you trust in two things: a) you can learn from whatever comes down the road and b) you'll adapt and make the best of whatever life offers.

Here's a personal example. At one point, I had a friend who was running a conference. I was a new speaker on the circuit. I thought he'd include me as one of the conference speakers since I was already part of his organization.

But then, he did not include me because I did not have a following yet. Wow—this really hurt. And I felt betrayed. I lost so much energy to feeling upset. Eventually, I was able to transform the direction of my thoughts. I realized that losing this speaking opportunity was only one of many such opportunities in my future. I had to get over that one loss and trust that this is an abundant universe with many positive possibilities.

I affirmed for myself that Higher Power will put me into new situations. I have a firm principle: "I'll serve wherever I am." So I do NOT demand that things go my way. I have preferences, but I seek to flow with what life offers.

Power Questions: How can you convert "demands" into "preferences"? How can you give up grieving over expectations that go unfulfilled and then shake off the dust of disappointment? One part of this process is to learn to step forward with whatever is positive and with whatever you have at hand.

3. Approval

In a backhanded way, my father helped me move beyond the desperation of desiring approval. For years, my father often offered NO approval at all. In his mind, he had all the answers and whatever I was doing was wrong.

Almost as a self-defense, I originated the idea: "Approval is an occasional dessert."

I go with my own heart. If a project feels to me like it will serve others and that I'll enjoy creating it, then I go and make that project happen. I chose the word "creating" with care just now. Whatever I do, I'm creating something: a product that serves people, an idea that uplifts someone's thoughts, or a process that eliminates frustration.

At the same time, I also realize that whatever project I do, some people will really enjoy the work, and others will not. My sweetheart and I have a way to deal with rejection or disapproval. We have a process I titled "Celebrate Someone Disagrees." It is a reward that we give ourselves for having the courage to put our ideas and projects out into the world. Usually, my sweetheart gets something chocolate as her reward. I often get a new book.

Power Questions: How can you let go of your need for approval? How can you honor your own intuition and take action because it aligns with your heart . . . instead of trying to gain someone else's approval? Will you implement some form of "Celebrate Someone Disagrees" process? In this way, you take care of yourself and avoid the dread of rejection.

4. Resistance (including judgment)

We all resist something at some time. If I ask you to hold up your hand and then I press my palm to your palm, you'll naturally press back and resist.

But resistance can drain us of energy. I know some people who do not take an aspirin or an aspirin-alternative when they have a mild headache. But then I notice that they report that they feel drained. Why do they feel this way? They have been resisting the pain they were feeling. Resistance takes energy.

A big part of resistance is judgment. Often we judge that something is "not right." For example, Susan might say, "It's not right for friends to forget to call another friend on her birthday." If she doesn't get calls on her birthday, she'll judge her friends as being wrong and inconsiderate.

Instead of judging, it helps to pull back to a neutral place in your thoughts. Some people call this neutral place the "Observer Mind." In essence, you merely observe what is going on. You let go of quick judgments about people or the particular situation. You see how you can flow with it and adapt to it. One of my editors asked, "What if someone can't adapt?" I replied, "The truth is that calming down is often the starting point for getting new and better ideas of how to deal with a tough situation. If your mind is racing, your thoughts can tumble into a negative spiral. One solution is to take some deep breaths and pause. Such deep breathing is part of calming down and the process of "going to the

Observer Mind."

I am now going to share with you an extreme example of using the Observer Mind. Through my childhood, my father would lift me by my hair and slam me into walls. When I was fifteen, he again lifted me by the hair. Suddenly, I became quiet inside. I could clearly see a choice before me. Skilled in karate, I could hit my father, or I could show my physical power without sinking to his level. I punched the wall, leaving a hole in it. My father never grabbed me by the hair again.

By going to my Observer Mind, I chose the best action. I stopped the physical abuse and avoided further violence.

I share the above example primarily because it is memorable and makes my point. We can think better—and make better decisions—when we practice going to the Observer Mind.

Let's go further in defining this Observer Mind. I've already mentioned how the Observer Mind is a "neutral place." It is distinctly different from the Ego Mind, which is made of fear. Many of us, if we're candid, will say that we spend much of our time feeling bad because of the past and being worried about the future. That's the Ego Mind in action.

On the other hand, the Observer Mind comprises that part of you which is above the chatter of fear. It notices your thoughts but does not get all caught up in them.

So how do we get to the Observer Mind? As I suggested already, pausing and taking deep breaths quiets the body, and that process may also quiet the mind. People who meditate actually practice going to the Observer Mind.

Research has shown through fMRI technology that people who meditate literally change the structure of their brains. Long-term meditators experience happiness and a huge level of positive emotions in the left pre-frontal cortex of the brain. Simultaneously, their right pre-frontal cortex is quiet (which silences negative thoughts).

If you're not a meditator, you can still get to your Observer Mind. You have probably done so already but just didn't realize that you had. Perhaps, in the middle of a disagreement, you realized, for a moment, that saying one particular sentence (something like "You never stop for a moment and think about doing something to help me!") would escalate the conversation into a vicious argument. So you refrained from saying that sentence. Good work.

Practice deep breathing and quieting the body and then mind whenever possible. You could practice while standing in a line at a department store or while riding an elevator.

You might also consider looking into meditation, regular quiet time, Tai Chi, yoga, or prayer time.

Power Questions: How can you just "observe" what's going on? How can you take the negative charge out of your interpretation of something that is going on? How can you look on others as "different" instead of instantly labeling them as "wrong"?

5. Source of identity

One year, a long-time friend (over 30 years) just cut off all contact. I grieved a lot over this.

But then I realized that the universe had actually done me a favor. This person had never believed in my writing, and in fact, his disdain had been an energy-drain.

However, I did not feel the relief of not having this "negative friend" gone from my life. Why? Because for too long, I held an ultimately disempowering idea. I thought, as a source of my identity, that I was a good person because I demonstrated so much patience with friends that I had a number of long-term friendships.

But then I realized: Some friendships are like novels. Others are short stories. And some are just paragraphs.

I now realize that any friendship may end at any time. Not because people are wrong, but because they may be moving onward in different directions.

I no longer base my identity upon whether or not my friendships are long-lasting.

Be very careful about what you use as the source of your identity.

If you base your identity on the approval of others, you set yourself up to feel miserable.

Be careful, too, about basing your identity on your achievements.

I remember completing the first feature film that I directed. Sure, it felt great to finish. But I was also exhausted. Since that time, I've learned to enjoy the journey. I live more of my life in-the-process rather than resting and obsessing over what I've done. My accomplishments are like a wake behind a boat. They are simply one part of my life. They do not "drive the boat." I do my real living, not looking backward, but creating now — in this moment.

It's more fun being in the moment and enjoying the work and camaraderie with my team.

I've noticed some people living only for achievements; they get massively frustrated during the whole creation process. Instead, it helps to enjoy the journey.

So, what can you base your identity on?

Some of my clients have suggested these ideas:
- basic trust in yourself that you act in kind ways.
- trust that Higher Power cares for you and is guiding you for your good and the good of people you

meet.
- trust that you'll keep learning and adapting.
- trust that expressing love is a good and healthy way to "be in the world."

Power Questions: What are your current sources of identity? Are these no longer helping you? Upon what do you base your good feelings about yourself? Do you want to change your focus point? Are your sources of identity under your personal control, or do they belong to someone else?

Some Thoughts on How Unblocking Happiness Releases Your Charisma Power

Charisma is about personal energy. Above I talked about how F.E.A.R.S. (Fear, Expectations, Approval, Resistance, Source of Identity) can block your happiness. These blocks can drain your energy to a massive extent.

Not everyone succumbs to F.E.A.R.S., though. If you present two different people with a set of circumstances, one will wallow in complaints, and the other will find opportunities for happiness.

For example, I know a filmmaker who completed a feature film that did not perform well and did not bring in the hoped-for financial rewards. However, she had a positive response:

"We had three goals:
1) entertain and uplift people
2) further our careers
3) make money.

We got two out of three. And I've learned so much that I'll do better next time."

Give yourself the best chance at staying on an even keel and enjoying a life of calm and confidence. Learn to handle the blocks to happiness: fear, expectations, approval, resistance, and source of identity.

Remember, people gravitate to those who exude positive power.

Book VI
Enhance Your Happiness to Radiate Charisma

Do you feel overwhelmed? We all do at times. But if you have "blocks to your happiness" running rampant in your life, you're likely also dampening your charisma.

The following four topics will unleash your potential, help you feel at ease, and enhance your ability to radiate charisma. (I first explored these topics at my popular blog at www.BeHeardandBeTrusted.com)

1) Say YES to Yourself and NO to Needless Trouble
2) The Secret Capability that Makes You Really Attractive for Success and Love
3) Enjoy the Precious Now
4) How You Can Start On Your Dream Today

Let's move forward.

1) Say *Yes* to Yourself and *No* to Needless Trouble

Would you like more time for what you love and less trouble in your life? Would you like the energy to be good to other people? Then learn to heed your intuition through the Y.E.S. process:

Y – Yearn for Valuable Moments
E – Embrace "the Pause"
S – Support Yourself

1. Yearn for Valuable Moments

We all desire Valuable Moments: moments of love, kindness, friendship, fulfillment, success, and fun. However, it's almost as if many things are set up to needlessly distract us from the best in life.

Here's a personal example. I often hire contractors. Sometimes those contractors are friends. One of my friends was struggling to find work. We had worked together about ten years before, so I considered hiring "George" to do some work.

I called George to offer him the work, but he turned the whole conversation to how things were inconvenient for him. He told me that I had to figure out all of the project's details and then call him back. This was not the spirit of collaboration and cooperation that I was looking for.

Instead of dragging things out, I called the next morning and said, "George, we're still friends, and I know we can be supportive of each other. However, my personal pace, my personal tempo, is fast. I don't let things slow down my momentum. When I was talking with you, it did not feel collaborative. I'm sad to say that we do not have a match. I do not have work for you."

So I faced the music. Sure I felt sad and concerned about how my friendship with George might not survive my refusal to get encumbered with him. But I knew I had made the right decision.

Then and now I have a higher priority: I want more Valuable Moments in my life. I don't want needless trouble or complications. Therefore, I am willing to do a "positive confrontation"; I'm willing to express my personal truth (what my heart feels). I have learned that facing some discomfort now can avoid a LOT of discomfort later.

I heeded my intuition. I could sense that lots of conflict would arise with George. It was not worth it. It would drain my time and energy.

Instead of getting encumbered with George, I moved on. Soon I jumped into writing and finishing another book, *Success Secrets of Rich, Smart and Powerful People: How You Can Use Leverage for Business Success* (you can look inside this book at Amazon.com). I enjoyed the collaboration of a bunch of best-selling authors including Brian Tracy, Chip Conley, Patricia Fripp, Mark Sanborn, Noah St. John, and Tony Alessandra. I'm so glad that I avoided the energy-drain of working with George.

2. Embrace "the Pause"

Are you someone who says "yes" too quickly? When I say, "Embrace the Pause," I mean: Create time for you to think through the consequences of saying "yes" to taking on some task or activity.

How do you create a "pause?" When someone asks you to take on some task, say something like: "I hear that this is important to you. I'll need to check some details to see if it is possible for me to help in some way."

When you get back to the person, you can say, "[Original request] doesn't work for me. What I can do is _____." In this way, you are showing some support, yet you avoid making trouble for yourself.

For example, Susan was asked by her friend Mindy to subscribe to Mindy's e-newsletter. Susan wanted to be supportive, but she didn't want her inbox choked with a lot of extra email. So Susan said, "I'll send a tweet out about your project." In this case, Susan provided some support—not exactly what Mindy wanted—but Susan needed to make her own decisions and to protect her own time and energy.

3. Support Yourself

I help someone every day. Sometimes I'll provide a link for a new author so that she can self-publish her first eBook. At other times I'll call a friend and tell her that I believe in her and her talent. How do I have the time and the personal energy for supporting others? The reason is: I take care of myself. For example, I make sure to sleep enough by keeping a log. I also exercise daily.

I realize that I'm sharing some personal examples. That's because, in this book, I want to share principles that I live by.

Sure, I sometimes fall short of completing each task on my schedule. But I always take action toward fulfilling my values.

Now, it's your turn. I invite you to get clear about your personal values and take appropriate action. Part of that process consists of using the Y.E.S. system so that you say YES to yourself and NO to needless trouble.

Remember:

Y – Yearn for Valuable Moments
E – Embrace "the Pause"
S – Support Yourself

Some Thoughts on "Say YES to Yourself and NO to Needless Trouble" and Charisma

Charismatic people project ease in the way they walk and talk. How? They're not feeling overwhelmed. They have learned to "Say YES to Yourself and NO to Needless Trouble."

Have you ever said, "Damn! I knew this was going to be trouble!"? My clients have often reported that trouble occurs when they fail to listen to their own intuition. The truth is: We need to make space so that we can listen to our intuition.

Charismatic people have mastered "the pause." That is, they pause before they say yes to a request. On the other hand, people who seem frail and without charisma often say yes too quickly and too often. That's a quick way to feeling overwhelmed.

So how do we create the "pause"? When someone asks us to do something, we can say something like: "I hear that this is important to you. I'll need to check some details to see if it's possible for me to help in some way."

As I mentioned earlier, if you need to refuse a particular request, you can do it with both confidence and diplomacy. Consider saying, "[Original request] doesn't work for me. What I can do is____."

Being straight forward about what you will and will not do helps you express charisma. People learn that they can trust you, and they admire your internal strength. I've often heard movie stars during interviews praise their director. They say, "She's a good director. She always knows what she wants." In essence, actors, like most people, appreciate when a leader (or even a co-worker) is forthright, confident, and clear about details.

Expand your charisma by protecting your time and energy. Then, you'll walk and talk with ease. Rehearse the ways you can diplomatically get a "pause" so that you can reflect before you say yes to requests.

2) The Secret Capability that Makes You Really Attractive for Success and Love

Are you flexible? If plans go astray, do you roll with it, or do you fume? Successful people I have interviewed are flexible. They adapt well and quickly to anything that arises in life. In fact, one of the many things I appreciate about my sweetheart is she's flexible. So what does it take to be flexible?

- An abundance of personal energy
- The ability to focus on what is most important
- The ability to adapt and improvise

1. An abundance of personal energy

If you're tired, waiting in line can be torture. Perhaps you've looked around and seen other desperate souls looking exhausted and disgruntled.

So to be flexible and have the necessary personal energy, focus on the basics: good sleep, nutrition, exercise, and quiet time.

In addition, carefully choose to devote your time with those people who raise your spirits. And guard your time from "energy vampires"—those people who suck every smile and even the oxygen out of the room.

To be flexible, you need to be strong. And you need lots of personal energy. Be sure to nurture yourself so you will be capable of adapting to whatever arises.

2. The ability to focus on what is most important

Inflexible people often focus on the trivial as if it is life-and-death. On the other hand, flexible people target what is most important in life and let go of the rest.

For example, during a get-together at a restaurant, one of my friends, "Kenneth," ordered one of the specials—a bacon tostada. Kenneth said that he usually avoided meat but this was going to be a treat. When the server returned and said there was no bacon left, my friend was flexible and suggested that the cook add guacamole in the place of the missing bacon.

Kenneth didn't complain about "false advertising." Instead, he looked for alternative solutions. He said, "What's important is that we friends are together. I'm fine with little changes in my meal."

To be flexible, you need to zero in on what is most important. Then you can shuffle ideas and possible solutions and find a way to create a good outcome.

3. The ability to adapt and improvise

In a way, I'm lucky. I made my first film when I was 9-years-old. What did I learn as a novice filmmaker? Tons. People don't show up. People can be stubborn. Film can get scratched. Special effects ideas can fail. But most importantly, I learned to adapt to anything on the set.

Now, whenever I begin a project, I accept that there will be both bumpy times and surprises along the way. I devise my own standards, or what I call criteria for excellence. I'm not looking for perfection. I choose what I feel is necessary for the project to turn out in an excellent way. By being able to improvise and to take in new ideas from team members, I find that every project turns out better than my first imaginings. How? My team members are comfortable with offering their own ideas, and they can see possibilities that I had not imagined when I first wrote the script.

Being flexible calls for adapting and improvising. Along these lines, it's good to get practice with responding to surprises. I find it helpful to listen first. While my team works to complete the graphic novel I wrote, *TimePulse*, I'm offered new ideas every day by the illustrators. Sometimes the new ideas directly contradict my first plan. It would be easy to react with a comment like: "No! That won't work." Instead, I take a breath and respond by asking, "Oh? So what's your reason for that detail?" On a number of occasions, I have accepted the new idea as an improvement to the graphic novel.

Some readers might ask, "So being flexible is about being good at compromising?" My answer is: "Compromising suggests losing something. I look on being flexible as having the ability to make adjustments—and still keep to your original intention. It's being strong enough to adapt."

As I mentioned above, being flexible includes these elements:
- An abundance of personal energy
- The ability to focus on what is the most important
- The ability to adapt and improvise

Consider the people you like to work with and the friends you have fun with. They are flexible people—yes? We are all looking for someone we can trust–whether we're talking about business or personal relationships. However, it's hard to trust someone who fails to be flexible. If "any little thing" can throw a person off, then we can't trust that person to come through with commitments—both business and personal.

When possible, look for flexible people. And aim to be flexible yourself. You'll do better in business by building your effective personal brand as someone who is capable, consistent, and flexible.

Some Thoughts on "Being Flexible" and Charisma

A friend was telling me about how he longed to find someone to love. As he described the traits of his perfect love, I thought of one more to add: "flexible." Flexible people are attractive and thus charismatic because they are the ones who adapt well to tough situations. A person who shows "grace under pressure" is attractive. Calmness is also a form of charisma. Grace under pressure also requires flexibility.

Rigid people bring trouble upon themselves. They do not truly listen to new ideas or possible solutions. How can you trust someone to lead a group when he cannot entertain new ideas? The answer is: You can't.

Good leaders are great listeners. They demonstrate flexibility and restraint when listening to ideas that may seem strange or unfeasible.

Good leaders find that every day brings new changes and new problems. Albert Einstein said, "You cannot solve a problem on the same level of consciousness in which it was created." In other words, in order to solve a problem, a leader either needs to shift to a resourceful level of consciousness, or she needs to get input from the consciousnesses of others. It is this form of flexibility that team members respect.

Charismatic people demonstrate their flexibility in how well they listen. They also assure others when they say something like: "That's interesting. I've haven't thought about it that way before. I'll think about it and get back to you this afternoon."

On the other hand, rigid people often say, "That won't work" and quickly dismiss a new idea—and the person proposing the idea. Here's the truth: if you quickly dismiss someone's ideas, that person will probably shut down emotionally. And he may never offer a new idea again. Why would he take the risk of emotional pain?

On the other hand, the charismatic person creates a positive environment in which people feel safe to make a contribution of ideas and efforts.

Be flexible; be trusted; and be appreciated.

3) Enjoy the Precious Now

Don't miss your life! When is it? Now. That's what we have. Sure, you can go into a fantasy of the future. You could imagine great things. Of course, sometimes imagining is helpful, such as when you create a vision for a particular project. However, here's the key: Create a vision for the future, but do not live there.

And be careful about the past as well. You can easily disappear into past regrets that you cannot right or even past joys that cannot be recreated.

Do not miss this Now-moment. Use the L.I.V.E. process to enjoy the precious now:

L – Love
I – Intuit
V – Value
E – Enjoy

1. Love

What do we really have in this world? Love. The love we express and the love that embraces us. You can experience this with people. Also, many of us sense a spiritual level of love.

Other people may say that they do not have love in their lives. What then? If your soul cries out for love . . . if you feel lonely, then find some way to express love to others. One of my favorite quotes in this vein is:

"If you want others to be happy, practice compassion.
If you want to be happy, practice compassion."
— The Dalai Lama

I make it a daily practice to say kind words to people who come my way. For instance, I'll express kindness in little comments I share with people I'm connected to on Facebook.

Express love and kindness. You'll lift other people's hearts and lift your own heart, too.

2. Intuit

Where are the answers to whatever situation you find yourself in? Your rational mind may provide a few. Other answers you need to listen for. Listen to your intuition.

But how exactly do you do that? It takes both practice and space.

For example, I may juggle my schedule to give myself quiet time before making some important decisions. At the moment, I'm completing TimePulse, the graphic novel, with a terrific team of illustrators, an associate art director, and more. I'm the writer and art director. If one of my illustrators shows me a wardrobe design for a character, I'll listen to the person's ideas, and then I'll say, "I'll stir that idea in my soup and get back to you."

Why do I wait to respond? Because I know from completing several creative projects, from a feature film to 40 books, that my intuition needs time. I need to clear some space. I know that I can work on something else for a bit and then return to the illustrations and I will feel the right answers. Further, my intention is to reach graphic novel readers on a feelings-level. So my rational mind cannot provide all the answers. And some rational ideas just don't have the gut-level power.

Intuition can provide the guidance for bringing in humor, too. As I teach graduate classes and give speeches, I also use intuition in the moment to create a memorable experience and relatable humor.

I invite you to make space for your intuition. Intuition provides opportunities for the extraordinary.

3. Value

Show that you value other people. Show how you appreciate the blessings they bring to your life. Every day, I thank someone—friends, family, team members of my company—for their efforts, diligence and kindness. When I'm teaching my online classes, I thank graduate students for posting their homework. I encourage them with my comments on their papers. I invite you to focus on your values and to put diligent effort into showing others that you value them and care about them.

4. Enjoy

Put effort into enjoying each day of your life. My father taught me this in a backward way. Now in his 70's, my father does not laugh much at all, and he does not smile for photographs, although he used to. He's not going forward; he's going backwards. In contrast, my hope is to gain more wisdom and more inner peace as I go through life.

So I've learned to live my life in an opposite manner than my father. I go out of my way to enjoy each day. I purposely seek out YouTube.com videos and standup comedy videos so that I enjoy humor and laughter each day. And I say funny things to get people near me to smile and laugh, too.

Why? It's to celebrate the Precious Now.

Our lives are made of each Now-moment–one after another.

Step forward and embrace each Now-moment.

Remember: Love, Intuit, Value, and Enjoy.

Some Thoughts on "Enjoy the Precious Now" and Charisma

People who are enjoying the present moment are more attractive because we are drawn to people who radiate positive energy. On the other hand, we are instantly repelled by doomsayers.

How do you enjoy the present moment? You learn to shake off a disappointment and return to a quiet confidence and warm energy. You have two powerful tools to help you with this: how you move and how you think. I'm referring to your habitual thought patterns, that is, those thoughts that repeat in your mind on a daily basis. For example, one of my clients avoids saying, "Damn!" or "Clumsy!" if something spills while he's making lunch. He'll mildly say, "That's different." His habit is to under-react and avoid overreacting.

When you make good choices in moving and thinking, you open the door to radiating charisma. So how do you do this? We'll start with movement and posture. Good posture is vital for radiating charisma. With my practice of yoga, I find that I sit or stand tall more often during my day. At the computer keyboard, I take breaks to stretch, and such movement revs up my energy.

Another example: Sean Connery, the first actor to play James Bond in feature films, was said to move with grace. In fact, one of my clients said that he felt more confident when he envisioned himself moving with grace like Sean Connery as James Bond.

Now we move onto empowered thinking. You need to take care so that your habitual thoughts support your feeling alive in the present moment. Many of us have a habit of saying negative comments that bring us down like: "Why does this always happen to me?" or "With my luck, I'll just miss the train."

Instead, practice new thought patterns to bring up your emotional tone.

First, identify how you're feeling. If you're feeling out of sorts, ask yourself: "Am I feeling regret over the past or worrying about the future?" Often, we are not living IN this present moment. We're stuck in the past or fretting about the future.

Some of my clients some combination of the following words to focus their attention on the present moment:
- "Now."
- "What is here now?"
- "What do I see now?"
- "How does the person in front of me feel now?"
- "How am I feeling now"?

Trained fire fighters have learned a mantra to get them into the present moment: "Put the white stuff on the red stuff." By repeating this to themselves, they focus on what's important right now: putting the water on the fire.

Focus on what is present here and now. Release yourself from burdens of the past or future. Direct your attention to the present moment. Use your own mantra, whether it is "Now" or another phrase similar to those above. By coming alive in the present moment, you open yourself to unleashing your charismatic power.

4) How You Can Start on Your Dream Today

What's your dream? Do want to start a project, film, a book, something else? The important thing is to "work with what you have." We'll use the G.O. process:
G – get experience
O – organize "criteria for excellence"

1. Get experience
In creating film/video/music projects for over 20 years, I've noticed something: We always want more time and a bigger budget.

Having limits in time and budget mean one thing: Important choices must be made.

It's possible to have an advantage when facing tough and important choices. How? Working on many projects can give you an instinct for making decisions. After so many projects, I know when to switch gears and when to give people space to explore what they're doing.

So, I invite you to start small, right where you're at. Often, to be at the right place doing the right thing for a breakthrough, you need to do small projects. *If you're looking for a miracle, start something in motion.*

If you're a novice actor, have a friend take a consumer video camera and capture your performance of a monologue. If you like it, place it on YouTube.com. Why? You never know who may see your video and share it with someone else. For example, the pop manager, Scooter Braun, discovered Justin Bieber via YouTube, and took him to meet R&B singer Usher and Justin Timberlake. Justin Bieber's career took a leap forward at that point.

If you're a budding illustrator, pull out a sketch book and sketch something—anything that captures your attention.

Find your own way to show the world, in a small way, what you can do.

You'll gain experience and then you'll have a storehouse of insights and, perhaps, even a honed intuition to make your next project better.

On the other hand, I know some creative people who took the "short view" and gave up too soon.

Instead, picture your lifetime. Just imagine how you'll get better and better at your craft. Sometimes, the breakthrough happens in one year—or five—or ten. Enjoy the journey. With so much experience, you'll be ready for your breakthrough when it arrives.

2. Organize "criteria for excellence"

As I mentioned, for each project there are limits of time, budget and even the endurance of the participants. Often, "perfection" is a moving target—and it may not even be appropriate. What makes a perfect painting?

I once asked a successful author, "How do you know when a book is done?" He said something a bit off color: "How do you know when to urinate?"

Sure, he got some chuckles from the audience. But there

was a kernel of truth: The answer was "you just know!"

How do you know what to aim for when you do a project? First, take some quiet time. Write down what you choose as "criteria for excellence." Such criteria will include two things: a) what you decide is most important to be included in your project and b) what you assess as non-essential. Both elements are important. At the beginning of this section I talked about a fact: We always want more time and a bigger budget. Since there are limits, especially when you're starting out, you need to devote your attention and efforts to what will make the best impact on your audience.

For example, I produce promotional films for my projects. To gain an investor or vital new team member, I need to introduce a project with maximum impact.

I've learned that keeping a promo film down to one-minute-long gets good results. Why? When I'm talking with someone on the phone and ask the person to view a *one-minute* video, *they tend to agree.*

So I've set as one criteria for excellence: "One minute." [See my video at Mayan Ruins and helmet diving under the sea at YouTube.com. Type into the Search box: "Tom Marcoux Mayan"]

Consider this other facet of setting your own criteria for excellence: You know when it's done. You aim to satisfy yourself. Why? No matter what you do—there's someone out there who will criticize it. And that's fine. It was not for them.

As I share with my graduate students, "At least satisfy yourself. If it moves you, it will move someone else."

Most importantly, start today with what you have. Why? It's really how you grow as a person and as an artist—whether your art is film or the life you lead.

Some Thoughts on How to Start On Your Dream Today—and Charisma

People who are making steady progress toward a personal dream are charismatic. Why? They radiate positive energy because they have a direction and they feel good about it!

"Your time is limited, so don't waste it living someone else's life. Don't be trapped by dogma—which is living with the results of other people's thinking. Don't let the noise of other's opinions drown out your own inner voice. And most important, have the courage to follow your heart and intuition. They somehow already know what you truly want to become. Everything else is secondary." — Steve Jobs

I know someone who said, "I'd like to get back the energy I had back in the '80s." My reply was: "You had a personal goal and you were working on it! Pick something today. And move forward."

Some of my clients have said, "I'm not sure what my personal dream is." One way to deal with this is to choose a goal of "I'm exploring." Each week do something to explore how you can express your personal natural brilliance. I call this: *Align with your design.* You have a unique makeup. Start exploring and expressing your creativity. Through this process, your charisma will be enhanced. You'll radiate that you're full of life, hope and positive possibilities.

Using Charisma for Top Performance in a Job Interview

"I really want this job," one of my former interns said, desperation in her voice. I asked if she wanted me to share with her the job interviewing techniques that I teach my graduate students in my Professional Communication class. She said, "Yes!" Now, I'll provide much of that training here for you.

We need charisma to stand out from the competition when we interview for a job. Specifically, we need Natural Charm Charisma and Warm Trust Charisma. As I mentioned at the beginning of this book, using three forms of charisma provides you with an advantage in both personal and business interactions.

Natural Charm Charisma includes things you can naturally do to make people comfortable in your presence. The goal is to get obstacles that block your charisma out of your way (like nervous hand gestures) and to let your natural charm shine through.

Warm Trust Charisma includes things you can do so that people feel that you're genuine and trustworthy. This form of charisma focuses on creating a warm connection.

Magnetic Charisma (Force of Nature) is overwhelming attractiveness.

Here, we will focus on Natural Charm Charisma and Warm Trust Charisma because you want to the interviewer to be comfortable with you. Why? Because an employer is really looking for those things in a candidate.

An employer wants a candidate who will:
1) fit well with the team
2) bring no trouble
3) demonstrate trustworthiness
4) prove capable of doing a great job
5) prove to be a "bargain"—that is, the candidate is so skillful that they bring much more value than the cost of their salary.

Over the years, I have trained groups at the California Employment Development Department and other groups like ProMatch (Sunnyvale, California). Further, I've coached clients and graduate/college students in effective job interview techniques. It is a joy to receive emails in which they happily report that they have obtained a job. Now, to gain the vital skills you need for a job interview, use the J.O.B. process:

J – Jump in with Natural Charm Charisma
O – Open with a story of strength
B – Bring truth about a weakness

1. Jump in with Natural Charm Charisma

You already have natural charm. Your mission then is to get obstacles out of your way so that you warmly radiate that charisma. First, you get nervous behaviors out of your way (as covered in other sections of this book). Second, you make sure that you're thoroughly prepared and have outlined your answers to interview questions so that you reduce anxiety. Now, we'll talk specifically about writing the outline of your answers to two crucial job interview questions.

Question #1: What is one of your strengths?
Question #2: What is one of your weaknesses?

First, let's focus on my suggestion that you "outline your answers." I am not inviting you to write a perfect script and then memorize the script word for word as your answer to these crucial job interview questions. Why? Such a rote response sounds forced and phony. That is the exact opposite of expressing your Natural Charm Charisma. Instead, you want to be real in the moment. You write a general outline of the main ideas you want to express. In the interview, you'll naturally vary some of the words you say while still getting your message across. As a result, you will sound real and truthful. You'll positively impress the job interviewer.

Secondly, you need to rehearse you answers to the crucial job interview questions. Do not merely go over your answers in your mind. You need to actually practice in front of someone you trust. Even calling them on the phone and practicing for just four minutes can provide you with much-needed experience.

2. Open with a story of strength

Job interviewers almost always ask candidates about their strengths. Yet I'm surprised at how ill-prepared interviewees are with such a question.

In reply, they say vague things like "I'm a team player" or "I get things done." That doesn't prove anything. That's just a statement. "It's not real until you tell a story," I say to the clients and students that I coach in effective communication. The reason is that you need to give the interviewer an experience of how you're the team player or how you get things done.

You provide that experience through a well-crafted story about your strength. What does such a well-crafted story have?

1) A Tough Problem that you faced.
2) Your Proposed Solution to the problem (the course of action that you suggested)
3) The Result (a Triumphant Ending to the situation).
4) An Endorsement from a supervisor, client, or co-worker.

An easier way to remember this pattern is
P.S.R.E. or
Problem - Solution - Result - Emotion

Here's an example of such a story. This is "Stephen's" response to the question, "What's one of your strengths?"

"At the time, I was a line producer for a feature film. The director was going over schedule and over budget. We still needed to film the meeting of the two romantic leads. The script called for them to meet on a city bus. That would require lots of extras, a bus rental, fees for off-duty police officers, and permits for the filming days—all very expensive. I suggested that the characters could meet in an elevator. We'd save more money by building the set in the living room of an apartment. The director and producer approved. The producer said, 'Stephen, I can always count on you to come up with a solution that saves the budget and takes good care of the film.'"

We notice that the above example ends with an endorsement from the producer. Here are other examples of endorsements:

- "And that's when my supervisor, Mark, said, 'I can always count on you, Samantha, to bring the project in under budget and before the deadline.'"
- "And that's when my client, Sarah, said, 'I don't how you do it, Maria. You always make the ad twice as good as my first ideas.'"

3. Bring truth about a weakness

If you respond well to the question "What's one of your weaknesses?" you can radiate Warm Trust Charisma. If you falter in your answer, you can destroy trust with the interviewers. For example, you could make a big mistake by following the faulty advice of some books on interviewing that suggest you make your weakness into some form of "hidden strength." They mistakenly suggest that you say something like: "I'm too detail-conscious." How is that a weakness? Trying to be too clever in your answer to the weakness question destroys the interviewers' trust. They are sophisticated and can see through "the game" you're playing.

As a business owner, I have hired many people. Over the years, I've also gained a number of jobs by acing the interview. I've learned that the following Weakness-Plus-Training Pattern really works for the "weakness question."

Weakness-Plus-Training Pattern for the Weakness Question

1) Admit to an "okay" weakness.
2) Tell how you got training or coaching to work on the weakness.
3) Describe what you do daily to handle the weakness.

1) Admit to an "Okay" Weakness

Once I asked a twenty-something job applicant about his weakness. He replied, "I'm lazy." He did not get the job. Laziness is not okay. So let's cover the bad weaknesses that you do not mention: a) being a night owl, b) procrastination, and c) "better doing work at the last minute."

So what can be an "okay" weakness? One example is: "At one time, I had trouble prioritizing my work." Another example is: "At one time, I had difficulty in speaking up in team meetings."

2) Tell how you got training or coaching to work on the weakness.

It's important to the prospective employer that you are coachable. They want people who hit the ground running and who are fast learners. They also want people who are NOT arrogant. They want team members who seek to improve their skills. See how the following example expands upon an earlier one:

"At one time, I had trouble prioritizing my work. So I took a time management workshop. During it, I learned about the 80/20 rule. The idea was 20% of what we do is responsible for 80% of our best results."

3) Describe what you do daily to handle the weakness.

This is a crucial part of the Weakness-Plus-Training Pattern. You do not pretend that you have no troublesome tendencies. Instead, you demonstrate that, as a top professional, you are handling your difficulty. Now notice how this last part comes into play in the example:

"At one time, I had trouble prioritizing my work. So I took a time management workshop. During it, I learned about the 80/20 rule. The idea was 20% of what we do is responsible for 80% of our best results. Now, I keep a Post-It on my phone console that reads "80/20" to remind me to set good priorities. In fact, I write a list of the next day's priorities before I leave work at the end of my current workday."

Be Prepared for a "Personal Brand" Question

The essence of your personal brand is your answer to this question: *What are you best known for?*

Here are examples of answers:
- "I'm best known for creating logos that increase sales. I interview clients and discover what are the big benefits that people get from their product or service. Then I create a logo that has an emotional appeal."
- "I'm best known for asking effective questions so that my coaching client can discover what really moves her to action."

* * *

Remember, you can radiate charisma when you do proper preparation for your job interview. Be sure to outline your answers to the strength/weakness questions. Rehearse at least 9 minutes a day before your job interview. And better yet, come up with three stories for your strength and three possible weakness-related stories, and test them with some people you trust.

Getting a job is a full-time job. Be sure to set a schedule of outlining your answers to tough questions and how you'll answer them. Also, schedule your rehearsal time with trusted people you know. The more you prepare, the better you will do. Further, you'll discover the truth of my principle: Courage is easier when I'm prepared.

With excellent preparation, your charisma will shine through.

BONUS MATERIAL #1:

Stop Giving Your Power Away!

"That's it. I can't do it. I give up," my friend, Sarah, said.

After an extended conversation, I shared with her, "You're telling yourself a story—a story that's hurting you. It's a 'death story.' Here's what will help you: a *'life* story.'"

In essence, Sarah was letting the life drain out of her eyes. Why? She was caught up in fear. That was taking away her personal power.

What do people give their power away to? I've come up with an acrostic:

D – disappointment (fear)
E – expectations
A – avoidance of pain
D – dread of loss of approval

If the above contributes to our giving our power away, what's on the other side of this equation? *What is our power? Choice.* You might not choose your first thought that arises. But the question is: **What will you choose for your Second**

Thought?

Choosing your *Empowered Second Thought* is how you hold onto your power.
For my client, Sandy, the first thought is: "I don't have enough clients."
Here's an *Empowering Second Thought:* "I'm reaching out to qualified prospects every day."
This leads to Empowering Questions including:
How can I qualify prospects?
Where can I find qualified prospects?
Now we'll face and overcome that which drains life from us:

1. Disappointment (fear)

Why do we fear disappointment so much? Because it hurts. It rocks our sense of who we are and what we think our life is. What can we do with such fear? *Quiet it down enough to keep moving forward.*

As I write about InstaMaxPro.com ("Instantly get better; Maximize your life."), I'm interested in how we can make *a quick shift in our thinking and in our actions.* First, "call out" any self-sabotage behavior connected to fear of disappointment. Tell yourself: **"I'm strong enough to handle disappointment."**

Some people function under a subconscious-mind banner of "If I do nothing, then I won't be disappointed in my lack of talent and skill." We learn by doing. Disappointment will arrive even if we do nothing. I recall Tony Robbins' comment: "Life isn't boring; *you* are boring."

Do NOT let this form of disappointment creep up on you. Take effective action.

Now it's your turn. How will you acknowledge the

possibility for disappointment and still move forward?

2. Expectations

Do you *expect* people to always treat you fairly? Do you always get appropriate treatment? *There's a better plan: Be ready* to calmly and effectively work with people to get better outcomes. I saw this recently in a restaurant. One woman received a terminally tough piece of steak. She calmly and pleasantly asked for salmon to replace that "piece of leather." The restaurant manager was calm and pleasant in return and offered a free dessert and a discount on her meal.

We lose energy to expecting people to be better than they are. Author Eckhart Tolle pointed out that **true freedom** includes the element of "non-attachment." Non-attachment is about holding to preferences and not making everything a demand. If a family member does not jump to do a task, see if you can step forward with calm and gratitude for what does work in your life.

There's something better than "expectations"—Effort-Goals and Result-Goals. You separate your goals into Effort-Goals (like making five marketing calls) and Result-Goals (gaining two new clients this week). You can be proud of yourself for your own efforts.

Now it's your turn. How will you release yourself from "the tyranny of expectations"? How will you set up Effort-Goals so you are proud of your own actions?

3. Avoidance of pain

It's natural to seek to avoid pain. The truth is: Pain is coming so *choose what's most important to you*. Pain of disappointment is coming. Pain of loss is coming. Still, you can **avoid a lot of pain of regret** that you failed to take action!

A number of people lose energy to focusing on avoiding pain. Instead, *focus on getting stronger.*

Now it's your turn. What can you do to get stronger? How will you ensure that you have enough sleep and exercise–and good nutrition? What will you drop from your life that no longer empowers you?

4. Dread of loss of approval

Here's one of my favorite quotes:

"30% of the people will love you. 30% will hate you. 30% couldn't care less." – Gabrielle Reece

This means, no matter what you do, 60% of people you encounter are NOT with you. So do NOT let fear of loss of approval run your life. You could do everything right, and still there are people who will misunderstand you and your good intentions.

Instead, *you choose what means most to you and you take action to support your own values.* In that direction, you'll experience joy and personal fulfillment.

Now it's your turn. How will you go forward from this moment forward focused on what's best for you, regardless of the negative remarks from family or friends?

* * * * * *

In summary, many of us lose energy to concerns over the "D.E.A.D." elements of:

D – disappointment (fear)
E – expectations
A – avoidance of pain

D – dread of loss of approval

I've learned to assess the situation by asking: **"Does this strengthen me?"**

Certain elderly relatives are so negative and even abusive so I reduce my exposure to them.
Do you need to make tough decisions so you STOP giving your power away?
Instead, identify what *strengthens* you. Take action to have more of that in your life.
In this way you apply the *InstaMaxPro Difference*. ("Instantly get better; Maximize your life.")

An Insight for Your Enhanced Charisma:
The person who lives in a way that enhances personal power strides through the world with an energy that naturally attracts the attention of other people.

BONUS MATERIAL #2

How to Overcome Self-Sabotage

"I get so close and then I sabotage myself!" my new client Anna said. I've helped a number of clients and audience members release themselves from the stranglehold of self-sabotage.

We'll use the C.A.L.L. process:

C – call it out
A – arrange support
L – leverage your good actions
L – live using a "buffer"

1. Call it out

When I say, "call it out," I mean identify the behavior as self-sabotage. For example, I've met business owners who delude themselves and find anything (that is, ANYTHING) other than doing the marketing and selling that their business needs for surviving and thriving. The answer is for business owners to call it out: "I'm hesitating to make the follow-up phone call. I feel like doing some filing now. That would be self-sabotage. I'm stronger than that!"

When you call out the self-sabotage, you can ask an Empowering Question: "How can I be stronger than this—in this Moment?"

The answer may be as simple as: "I'll stand up now for this phone call" or "I'll have a drink of water."

When you call out some behavior as self-sabotage, you can look deeper. **I've noticed that self-sabotage can arise from fear.** In fact, some time ago, my sweetheart said, "Tom, what are you afraid of?" At the time, I didn't like the question, but then I noticed that when I *identified* the fear *its power diminished.* I could pull out a sheet of paper and identify what I could do to lessen possible impacts. For example, one time I experimented with holding a workshop in a far off city for the first time. I had people who were going to co-present. What was my fear?–that no one would attend. *What was my solution?* If no one attended, I'd call it a private coaching session for my co-presenters! *I would still deliver value to* my co-presenters. *I was ready* for a tough outcome. (By the way, people did attend and praised the event!)

Now it's your turn. What can you do to "call out" and label self-sabotage when it rises up in your day?

2. **Arrange support**

Some people think that it's somehow noble to "go it alone." Really? What if you're sick? Is it smart to get no help? No accurate diagnosis and no life-saving medication? Certainly, we realize the value of getting appropriate help from a doctor.

As an Executive Coach and the Spoken Word Strategist, I help people rise above and become even better than their first imaginings. Realize this: No Olympic athlete competes without a coach. None! I know, I'm the Executive Coach to a sports psychologist who has coached several gold medalists.

Picture this. When you want to stretch your legs, you use something as support—a chair, the floor, or a barre (that's the handrail that a ballerina uses).

With my clients, I provide well-timed questions to help them uncover unique ways for them to stretch and have the support in their lives they need.

Now it's your turn. How will you arrange support in your own life? Who can coach you so you take action that is BETTER than old, self-defeating patterns? (Support can be a friend who takes walks with you—or even a therapist who helps you release old pain and step forward in life.)

3. Leverage your good actions

Leverage is about putting in a small amount of effort and getting big, valuable results. You could use a lever and move a boulder. That is, if you put the fulcrum in the right place, you'd only need to use a small bit of effort.

When I'm talking about "leverage your good actions," I'm talking about adopting a winning mindset. Such a winning mindset is the combination of well-placed fulcrum and lever. For example, successful people I've interviewed emphasize the value of follow-up. Many people find follow-up to be a chore. I've emphasized with my clients, a better approach. I call it *"Follow-Good."* It begins with the question: "How can I make this a good interaction for the other person and me?" You look for ways to be a welcome presence in other people's lives.

Using "Follow-Good" transforms follow-up calls into something positive in your life.

Even if someone may not become a client, they get value from talking with you so they become a good source of referrals.

Let's take this further. What are you already doing that works well in your life? See if you can expand on that. For example, I eat salad for breakfast. Research at Stanford University shows that one's willpower is strongest, early in the day. So I take no chances! — I eat salad when I feel strong.

Now it's your turn. How can you focus on what you're doing well and expand your positive actions from there?

4. Live using a "buffer"

One synonym for "buffer" is "cushion"—and we've heard the phrase "Give yourself a cushion of time." Here we'll take this idea a step further.

I've described the process to my clients in this way:

"Imagine a ruler with "A" marking one inch. "B" is two inches. And so forth. You're at point "A"—you stretch to your right past points B, C, and D. Now pull back to point C. Why? To give yourself a 'buffer' or 'cushion.' You need a reserve of energy. (Yes, that's the space between C and D.) If point D is the edge of your energy, that's a danger point. Instead, always seek to have a reserve of energy because tough surprises occur."

If you stretch yourself too thin, you're on the edge of disaster. Do NOT let this happen.

Make sure you supply your buffer (or cushion) with enough sleep, exercise, good nutrition and quiet time each day.

Authors and researchers have noted:

- Tired people make mistakes.
- Tired people avoid taking appropriate risks (Why? They don't have the energy.)
- Tired people do not have the brain capacity to be aware of surprise opportunities.

Letting yourself live on the edge without enough sleep (for example) is truly self-sabotage.

Here's another vital point: **You need to have some "pure fun" in your life.** Why? Because when you live only a harsh, overly-disciplined life, it is likely that your inner child (the source of your energy) is going to eventually "act out."

What is "acting out"? It can be any of the self-sabotage-behaviors including:
- Binging with food, TV, video games and something else
- Getting angry and treating someone in a harsh manner
- Taking bad risks (including unprotected sex, for example)

Take care of your inner child, then you can avoid that part of you "acting out."

Your inner child wants to "be heard." And your inner child wants some fun—and time off!

Now it's your turn. How will you take better care of yourself? How would you treat yourself better—as if you were caring for a close friend? Take out a journal and write down "Inner child, what do you want?" Note your answers. (I just did this. And as soon as I complete this article, I'm going to watch a couple scenes from one of my favorite, silly movies from my collection of various films.)

* * * * * *

Remember, call out your self-sabotage-behaviors. Do what's necessary to keep yourself strong.

An Insight for Your Enhanced Charisma:
When you free yourself of self-sabotage-behaviors, you have more energy. Such energy attracts the attention of other people.

BONUS MATERIAL #3

Be Your Mighty Self

"I can't do that," my client Beverly said.
"Really? Who makes the rules?" I asked.
In my work as an *Executive Coach and the Spoken Word Strategist,* I encounter clients who have allowed somebody's limiting ideas to become their own. Often, *a simple, powerful question can make the real difference.*
Ask yourself:
What would my Mighty Self do?

First ... who is your Mighty Self? It's that part of you that is naturally brilliant and courageous.
On the other hand, so many of us, live too much of the time in our ego, which is made of fear.
The answer is to **condition yourself to shift out of your first fearful thoughts.**
I talked with "Janet," a new author — and I asked her, "How about you ask [best-selling author] to consider giving you an endorsement for your book?"

"No. That best-selling author won't listen to me. That author won't care," Janet replied.

"How do you know?" I asked.

"Well … I guess I don't know for sure," Janet said.

"Who is talking, when you said, 'that author won't listen to me'?" I asked.

"I don't … I guess I'm thinking of my father who said, 'You're no good at that,'" Janet replied.

"Okay. I hear that," I began. "We need you to connect with *something else. Somebody else.* Here's a whole, different point of view for you. Listen carefully. **What would Your Mighty Self do?"**

Janet paused. Then her eyes got wider, and she said, "My Mighty Self would make the call and would send the email. Or reach out on Facebook."

"That's right!" I said, full of enthusiasm.

To Connect with Your Mighty Self, You Need a Powerful Source of Energy

Recently, I heard someone say, "This is the best day of my life."

How about that? What would be part of YOUR best day in life?

- Who would you be with?
- What would you be doing?
- What would be so exciting?
- What would be fun?
- What pulls you forward?

Sometimes, I ask, "What's shiny?" And then I say, "That's your Golden Pull Goal. It pulls you forward. It's a powerful source of energy.

How are you going to make a Best Day happen?

Actually, in my work with clients, I do not emphasize a whole day. I invite my client to create **"many happy moments."** One client imagined feeling the moments of joy seeing his daughter's delighted face—walking into Disneyland.

Your Mighty Self is Ignited by "Best Day Details"!

A Secret for a Certain Group of Individuals:

Think of someone you care about. A romantic partner or friend or family member.

What would make up the best day for that loved one's life?

Now, you have something interesting to work with and to create with.

Some of us are hard-wired as a "for-the-team" person (that's my term). That is, *you'll do much more for a loved one than for oneself.* If that's you, put that truth to full use. By this I mean, you connect with Your Mighty Self by tying something great for a loved one with your business goals.

It can be as simple as "20% of every sale I make goes to my daughter's college fund."

Or ... we'll launch this new product and devote a portion of the income from sales so I can take my wife on that Alaska-cruise she wants so much.

Your Mighty Self is about Positive Possibilities and Shaking Free of Fear.

If your first thought arises from fear with: "I don't know how to do this. Even if I try, it will fall apart" ... **then condition yourself to have an** *Empowered Second Thought.*

Such Empowered Second Thoughts can be:
- I can learn whatever I need to learn.
- I can adapt and come back stronger and better.
- I have a Mighty Purpose and I'm strengthened by the Good in the Universe

My friend, you are NOT stuck.

You do have new opportunities ahead.

You can focus on Your Mighty Self.

Years ago, the song belted out by Mighty Mouse included: "Yes! I've come to save the day!"

Make *your* day better.

Remember … **What would my Mighty Self do?**

Then take empowered action.

An Insight for Your Enhanced Charisma:

When you're able to shift your focus to *living from your heart* (away from fear), you radiate charisma.

BONUS MATERIAL #4:

Do you need a "Leap Forward" Idea for Success?

"I need to get unstuck. I know that I could be living on a higher level of success and happiness," my client Amanda said.

"I hear you," I replied. At a certain point in our conversation, I asked, "Would you like to hear a little surprising idea that I learned from one of my mentors?"

"Sure," Amanda said.

"Take a couple of ideas that you like individually. Then try some combinations," I said. We went through a number of combinations. Amanda found some new ideas by trying this process.

Some time ago, I helped another client, Deborah, as I asked her this series of questions:
- Who do you want to help?
- What's fun for you?
- Where do you want to go—that would be fun?

- How can you help some people heal and heal a part of yourself?

Based on her responses, I said, "It sounds like you want to guide women at a conference in Hawaii!"

"Yes! That would be ... amazing!"

I call this process a "Combo-Miracle." You combine ideas. Sometimes, you juggle the order.

Recently, I wanted to rename a keynote speech that I give at conferences and more.

One of my mentors, Jack Zufelt, known as the "Mentor to Millions", suggested that I look at my books and combine some elements of the titles. In that spirit, I combined two titles of books I've written *Soar! Nothing Can Stop You This Year* and *The Power of Confidence.* [If you're curious, you can read portions of those books on Amazon.com.]

What is the new speech title I now have? **"Soar with Confidence."**

This process works for other decisions. For example, in a particular family, some wanted a vacation of hiking in the mountains, and other family members wanted to swim in the ocean. The Combo-Miracle solution was Hawaii—swimming and hiking available!

Now it's your turn. How can you use this process of a "Combo-Miracle" in your life?

An Insight for Your Enhanced Charisma:
When you're taking action on Leap Forward Ideas, you feel excited about your life. Then, you truly radiate charisma.

BONUS MATERIAL #5:

Use the Real Secret to More Prosperity

"What will make a breakthrough for me to have more prosperity?" my client Anne asked.

I introduced her to what I call "On Time Airport Commitments (OTA)."

"People who call themselves average have a form of commitment that they always complete," I said.

"What?" Anne asked.

"They are **on time** to get on a plane at the airport," I continued.

Getting to the airport on time, for many people, is a "special commitment." A number of individuals will be late for lunch with a friend, but they will be on time to avoid missing their flight.

The truth is: **The successful people I've interviewed have more commitments in their personal "OTA Commitments box."**

I've noticed that I've put more daily commitments into my OTA box including: sit-ups, pushups, using a sinus rinse, writing a certain number of words per day and more.

My clients have placed these actions into their OTA Commitments box:
- Walk 10,000 steps per day
- Make 10 marketing phone calls a day (five days a week)
- Thank one's spouse every day for something
- Praise one's girlfriend about something each day

A special note: *How do you choose what to be an OTA Commitment?* First connect to what you want—deep in your heart. Identify what daily actions will manifest what you want.

As an Executive Coach, I help my clients create more success AND fulfillment. **I take them from "cloudy" to clarity. I ask well-selected questions.** I often ask "what"-questions and **not** "why" questions. I've observed that when you ask why, in response the person jumps out of their heart and into their head to deliver an answer that "sounds good."

Instead, I ask:
- What do you really want?
- When you're doing that [action], what will you feel?
- What feels good about that?
- What do you get from that?

Now it's your turn. What do you really want? What OTA Commitment (daily action) will get that for you?

An Insight for Your Enhanced Charisma:
I've observed that people who radiate charisma are those who fulfill their commitments. They trust themselves, and other people easily trust them, too!

A Final Word and the Springboard to Your Dreams

Congratulations on your efforts with this book.
We have explored the three forms of charisma:

Natural Charm Charisma includes things you can naturally do to make people comfortable in your presence. Your goal is to get obstacles out of our way (like nervous hand gestures) and let your natural charm shine through. *The image: Take a cover off a glowing light bulb.*

Warm Trust Charisma includes things you can do so that people feel that you're genuine and trustworthy. It's all about a warm connection. *The image: Your hand extends in friendship.*

Magnetic Charisma (or Force of Nature) is overwhelming attractiveness. *The image: A magnet pulls people in.*

I am glad to provide these insights so you can leap

forward to making your dreams come true.

Please consider gaining special training through my coaching (phone and in-person), workshops and presentations. Visit my blog:

PitchPowerFest.com
BeHeadandBeTrusted.com
InstaMaxPro.com
YourBodySoulandProsperity.com

Consider the other eight books in this series. . .

- Darkest Secrets of Persuasion and Seduction Masters: How to Protect Yourself and Turn the Power to Good
- Darkest Secrets of Negotiation Masters: How to Protect Yourself …
- Darkest Secrets of Making a Pitch to the Film and Television Industry
- Darkest Secrets of Business Communication: Using Your Personal Brand
- Darkest Secrets of Small Business Marketing
- Darkest Secrets of Spiritual Seduction Masters
- Darkest Secrets of the Film and Television Industry Every Actor Should Know
- Darkest Secrets of Film Directing

Meanwhile, to get even more value from this book, take the plans and insights that you created and place them in some form in your calendar or day planner. *Plan and take action.* Return to these pages again and again to reconnect with the material and take your life to higher levels.

The best to you,
Tom
Tom Marcoux

Executive Coach and Spoken Word Strategist
Pitch Coach
Special Offer Just for Readers of this Book:
Contact Tom Marcoux at tomsupercoach@gmail.com for special discounts on **coaching**, books, workshops and presentations. Just mention your experience with this book.

Excerpt from
Darkest Secrets of Persuasion and Seduction Masters: How to Protect Yourself and Turn the Power to Good
by Tom Marcoux, Executive Coach – Spoken Word Strategist
Copyright Tom Marcoux

. . . Now, I am in my 40's, with gray in my hair, and for 27 years I have been taking action to protect people.

And now is the time for me to protect you with the Countermeasures I reveal in this book.

Every human being needs to be able to break the trance that a Manipulator creates. You need to make good decisions so you are safe and you keep growing—and you are not cut down and crippled.

This Darkest Secrets material is so intense that I first released it only with the counterbalance of my most energizing and uplifting books, *Nothing Can Stop You This Year!* and *10 Seconds to Wealth: Master the Moment Using Your Divine Gifts.*

An interviewer asked me: "Who can be the Manipulator?"

A co-worker, a boss, a salesperson, someone you're dating, and someone you think is a friend.

Now is the time—this very minute—for me to write this book to protect you.

I must speak the truth.

These Darkest Secrets of "persuasion masters" are …

Wait a minute! Let's say it plainly: These are the Darkest Secrets of masters of manipulation. Throughout this book, I will call these people what they are: Manipulators.

Dictionary.com defines "manipulate" as "To influence or manage shrewdly or deviously.… To tamper with or falsify for personal gain."

In this book, we will look on a manipulator as one who deviously influences someone with no concern about that person's well-being, and who causes harm to that person.

Here is the first Darkest Secret:

Darkest Secret #1:
Manipulators Make You Hurt
and Then Offer the Salve.

Manipulators would invite you to go out in the sun for hours and then sell you the salve to soothe your burns. The problem is that we don't notice that this is what they're doing.

For example, you're considering the purchase of a house. A Manipulator asks the question, "So, where would you put your TV?" This question is designed to put you into a trance.

Dictionary.com defines "trance" as "a half-conscious state, seemingly between sleeping and waking, in which ability to function voluntarily may be suspended." Let's condense this: in a trance you may not be able to function freely.

Here is the second Secret:

Darkest Secret #2:

Manipulators Put You into a Trance.

To protect yourself, you must learn to use Countermeasures to Break the Trance.

All the Countermeasures (actions you can take to break the trance) in this book will make you stronger and more capable of protecting yourself.

Now, we'll view the third Secret:

Darkest Secret #3:

Manipulators Care Nothing for You and Human Decency: They'll lie, cheat, and do whatever they need to do so they win—but their charm masks all this.

Let's return to the example of a Manipulator selling you a house. A Manipulator does not pause for an instant to see if you can truly afford the new house. The Manipulator would neglect to mention that you will not only have your mortgage payment of $900. There will be additional costs: home repairs, property tax, water, electricity, homeowner's insurance, and more. The Manipulator only emphasizes what he or she knows you want to hear: "Look! $900 is better than the $1500 you're paying for rent, which is just going down the toilet. And the $900 is an investment."

Let's go back to **Darkest Secret #1:**

Manipulators make you hurt and then offer the salve.

The Manipulator has you feeling good about the solution (salve) and feeling bad about your current life situation.

How? A Manipulator will make you hurt through

questions such as:

- What bothers you about paying $1500 a month for rent? (The Manipulator will use a derisive tone when he says the word rent.)
- What is not smart about paying rent on someone else's house instead of investing in your own house?
- How do you feel about your children walking in the neighborhood where you live now?

Do you see how these questions are designed to make you hurt enough so that you'll buy?

An interviewer asked me, "Tom, aren't these good arguments for purchasing a house?"

"What we're looking at is the *intention* of the influencer," I replied. "Let's look at our definition of a manipulator as one who deviously influences someone with no concern about that person's well-being, and who causes harm to that person. If the person truly cannot afford the house, he or she will be harmed by buying it. If the manipulator conceals the truth, the manipulator is doing harm. That's the important difference."

Some friends of mine are ethical and helpful real estate agents who truthfully reveal the whole situation and help the purchaser achieve her own goals.

In this book, we are talking about another type of person; that is, unethical Manipulators.

* * *

In any given moment, we need to remember the tactics Manipulators use. We will focus on the word D.A.R.K. so you can remember details easily and protect yourself from Manipulators.

D — Dangle something for nothing

A — Alert to scarcity

R — Reveal the Desperate Hot Button

K — Keep on pushing buttons

1. Dangle Something for Nothing

What do conmen and conwomen do to seize your attention? They make you think you're getting a "steal."

I recently saw a documentary in which a conman on a street in England showed a toy that looked like it was dancing. This fake product was actually dancing because of a hidden, invisible thread. The conman was dangling something for nothing. The Entranced Buyer thought he was getting something worth $20 for only $5. That was the trick. The Entranced Buyer felt that he was getting $15 extra of value for his $5. What the Buyer really got was something worth nothing. Similarly, I know someone who purchased a copy of a Disney movie from a street vendor in San Francisco. She brought the copy home and it was unwatchable—and the street vendor was never seen again.

An old phrase goes, "A conman cannot con someone who is not looking for something for nothing."

How to Protect Yourself from "Dangle Something for Nothing"

Stop! Get on your cell phone and talk through the "deal" with someone you know who thinks clearly. Go home. Think about it. Do some research on the Internet. Listen to your gut feelings. If the salesman or conman is too insistent, get away from that Manipulator. Get quiet. Have a cup of water. Cool down. Break the Trance!

Break the Trance and Identify the Crucial Detail

Earlier, I mentioned that a Manipulator puts you into a trance. An added problem is that we put ourselves into a trance. For example, as you read this, are you thinking about your right toe? Most likely not (unless you stubbed your toe recently). The point is that we only focus on a tiny percentage of what is going on in our life.

Around fifteen years ago, I caused myself trouble because I put myself into a trance. I discovered that under certain conditions, friendship can make you nearly deaf. Here's how: I was producing a song for a motion picture. A good friend was singing backup in the chorus. Because of our friendship, I wanted him to sound great. I completely missed the Crucial Detail. In this kind of situation, the Crucial Detail is that what truly counts is how the lead singer sounds! I made a song that I could not release. What a waste of time and money! I had put myself into a trance.

In any situation in which the Manipulator is "dangling something for nothing," we often fall into a trance and miss the Crucial Detail. The most important detail is *not* that we're saving money if we order before midnight tonight. What counts is whether the product creates a lasting, crucial benefit in our lives. And is the benefit of the product worth the cost? Some people even program themselves to make mistakes by saying, "I can't pass up a bargain." The bargain is *not* the Crucial Detail.

Secrets to Break the Trance

This is the process of B.R.E.A.K.S. It will help you remember the proven methods to break a trance.

B — Breathe
R — Relax
E — Envision
A — Act on aromas
K — Keep moving
S — Smile

Secret #1: Breathe

Remember Secret #1: Manipulators make you hurt and

then offer the salve. The Manipulator wants to put you into a state of being that fills you with a sense of urgency and anxiety. Oh, no! I'm going to miss the sale!

Stop this highly vulnerable state. Take a deep breath.

End of Excerpt from
Darkest Secrets of Persuasion and Seduction Masters: How to Protect Yourself and Turn the Power to Good

Purchase your copy of this book (paperback or eBook) at Amazon.com or BarnesandNoble.com
See **Free Chapters** of Tom Marcoux's 40 books at http://amzn.to/ZiCTRj

ABOUT THE AUTHOR

You want more and better, right? Imagine fulfilling your Big Dream.

Tom Marcoux can help you—in that he's coached thousands of people: CEOs, small business leaders, graduate students (at Stanford University) speakers, and authors.

Marcoux is known as an effective **Executive Coach** and **Spoken Word Strategist.**

(and Thought Leader—okay, writing 40 books helped with that!)

** *CEOs, Vice-Presidents, Other Executives, Small Business Leaders:*

You know that leading people and speaking at your best can be tough.

Marcoux solves problems while helping you amplify your own Charisma, Confidence and Control of Time.

Interested? Email Marcoux—tomsupercoach@gmail.com

Ask for a *Special Report:*

* 9 Deadly Mistakes to Avoid for Your Next Speech

** *Speakers, Experts—for a great TED Talk, Book, Audio Book, Speeches, YouTube Videos.*

Marcoux solve problems while helping you to make your Concise, Compelling Message that gets people to trust you and get what you're offering (product, service, *an idea*).

Marcoux is the founder of **PitchPowerFest.com**

Yes—the *San Francisco Examiner* designated Tom Marcoux as "The Personal Branding Instructor."

As a **Pitch Coach**, Marcoux is an expert on STORY. He won a Special Award at the EMMY AWARDS, and he directed a feature film that went to the CANNES FILM MARKET and earned international distribution.

(Marcoux helps you *be heard and be trusted*—a focus point of his 16th Anniversary edition book, *Connect: High Trust Communication for Your Success in Business and Life*.)

As a CEO, Marcoux leads teams in the United Kingdom, India and the USA. Marcoux guides clients & audiences (IBM, Sun Microsystems, etc.) in "Soar with Confidence", leadership, team-building, power time management and branding. See Tom's Popular BLOG:

www.TomSuperCoach.com

Specialties: coach to CEOS * Executives * Small Business owners * Leaders * Speakers * Experts * Authors * Academics

One of his *Darkest Secrets* books rose to #1 on Amazon.com Hot New Releases in Business Life (and in Business Communication). A member of the National Speakers Association for over 15 years, Marcoux is a professional coach and guest expert on TV, radio, and print.

Marcoux addressed National Association of Broadcasters' Conference six years running. With a degree in psychology, he is a guest lecturer at **Stanford University**, DeAnza, & California State University. Over the years, Marcoux has taught business communication, designing careers, public speaking, science fiction cinema/literature and comparative religion at Academy of Art University. He is engaged in book/film projects *Crystal Pegasus* (children's) and *Jack AngelSword* (thriller-fantasy). See Tom's well-received blogs at

BeHeardandBeTrusted.com
PitchPowerFest.com
YourBodySoulandProsperity.com
InstaMaxPro.com

Consider engaging **Tom Marcoux as your Executive Coach.**

"As Tom's client for many years, I have benefited from his wisdom and strategic approach. Do your career and personal life a big favor and get his books and engage him as **your Executive Coach.**" – Dr. JoAnn Dahlkoetter, author of *Your Performing Edge* and Coach to CEOs and Olympic Gold Medalists

"Tom Marcoux coached me to get more done in 10 days than other coaches in 2 years." – Brad Carlson, CEO of MindStrong LLC

As the Spoken Word Strategist, Tom Marcoux can help you with **speech writing** and **coaching for your best performance.**

As the founder of **PitchPowerFest.com** and as a **Pitch Coach**, Tom trains CEOs, entrepreneurs and business owners to make **compelling pitches** to gain funding, key team members and powerful advisors.

As Tom says, *Make Your Speech a Pleasant Beach.*

Join Tom's Linkedin.com group: *Executive Public Speaking*

and Communication Power.

At Google+: join the community "Create Your Best Life – Charisma & Confidence"

Get a **Free** report: "9 Deadly Mistakes to Avoid for Your Next Speech and 9 Surefire Methods" at http://tomsupercoach.com/freereport9Mistakes4Speech.html

Tom Marcoux has trained CEOs, small business owners, and graduate students to speak with impact and gain audiences' tremendous approval and cooperation. *Learn how to present and get thunderous applause!*

"Tom, Thanks for your coaching and work with me on revising my speech at a major university. Working with you has been so enlightening for me. Through your gentle prodding and guidance, I was able to write a speech that connects with the audience. I wish everyone could experience the transformation I have undergone. You have helped me discover the warm and compelling stories that now make my speech reach hearts and uplift minds. This was truly an empowering experience. I cannot thank you enough for your great assistance." — J.S.

- **"Tom Marcoux has been an NAB Conference favorite [speaker] for six years. And he is very energetic." – John Marino, Vice President, National Assn. of Broadcasters, Washington, D.C.**

- **"Using just one of Tom Marcoux's methods, I got more done in 2 weeks than in 6 months." – Jaclyn Freitas, M.A.**

Tom's Coaching features innovations:
- Dynamic Rehearsal
- Power Rehearsal for Crisis
- The Charisma Advantage that Saves You Time

Become a fan of Tom's graphic novels/feature films:

- Fantasy Thriller: *Jack AngelSword*
  type "JackAngelSword" at Facebook.com

- YA Fiction: *Jenalee Storm*
  At Facebook.com type: "JenaleeStorm"

- Science fiction: *TimePulse*
  www.facebook.com/timepulsegraphicnovel

- Children's Fantasy: *Crystal Pegasus*
  www.facebook.com/crystalpegasusandrose

See **Free Chapters** of Tom Marcoux's 40 books at http://amzn.to/ZiCTRj   Amazon.com

www.ingramcontent.com/pod-product-compliance
Lightning Source LLC
Chambersburg PA
CBHW060523100426
42743CB00009B/1413